The Innovative Management Education Ecosystem

With the world in the midst of the Fourth Industrial Revolution, associated labor market challenges are bringing changes to how business schools offer executive education to the future workforce. The COVID-19 pandemic has further underlined the need for such change through impacts on today's workforce and the expected developments that ongoing technological advancements will have on the workforce of the future.

This book explores the need for business schools to strategically work to redefine the concept of an innovative business school ecosystem through commitment to experimentation and innovation. The authors advocate for such change to be realized through partnerships supporting actions that ensure graduates' and workers' access to skills building and reskilling and upskilling. The book presents selected case studies exemplifying such an approach and highlights best practices that can be implemented in public–private as well as private–private partnerships.

The Innovative Management Education Ecosystem: Reskilling and Upskilling the Future Workforce offers readers from industry and academia as well as government institutions insights that will benefit the development of innovative curricula and training programs and, at the same time, labor markets.

Jordi Diaz is the Dean and Professor of Innovation at EADA Business School Barcelona, Spain.

Daphne Halkias is a Professor and Distinguished Research Fellow at École des Ponts Business School in Paris, France.

Paul W. Thurman is a Professor of Management and Analytics at Columbia University's Mailman School of Public Health, New York, USA.

Routledge Focus on Business and Management

The fields of business and management have grown exponentially as areas of research and education. This growth presents challenges for readers trying to keep up with the latest important insights. *Routledge Focus on Business and Management* presents small books on big topics and how they intersect with the world of business research.

Individually, each title in the series provides coverage of a key academic topic, whilst collectively, the series forms a comprehensive collection across the business disciplines.

The Emptiness of Business Excellence
The Flawed Foundations of Popular Management Theory
David Collins and Jack Collins

The Innovative Management Education Ecosystem
Reskilling and Upskilling the Future Workforce
Jordi Diaz, Daphne Halkias and Paul W. Thurman

Management and Labor Conflict
An Introduction to the US and Canadian History
Jason Russell

Creativity, Innovation and the Fourth Industrial Revolution
The da Vinci Strategy
Jon-Arild Johannessen

Performance Measurement in Non-Profit Organizations
The Road to Integrated Reporting
Patrizia Gazzola and Stefano Amelio

For more information about this series, please visit: www.routledge.com/
Routledge-Focus-on-Business-and-Management/book-series/FBM

The Innovative Management Education Ecosystem

Reskilling and Upskilling the Future Workforce

Jordi Diaz, Daphne Halkias, and Paul W. Thurman

Routledge
Taylor & Francis Group

NEW YORK AND LONDON

First published 2023
by Routledge
605 Third Avenue, New York, NY 10158

and by Routledge
4 Park Square, Milton Park, Abingdon, Oxon, OX14 4RN

Routledge is an imprint of the Taylor & Francis Group, an informa business

Library of Congress Cataloguing-in-Publication Data
Names: Diaz, Jordi, author. | Halkias, Daphne, author. | Thurman, Paul W., author.
Title: The innovative management education ecosystem : reskilling and upskilling the future workforce / Jordi Diaz, Daphne Halkias and Paul W. Thurman.
Description: 1 Edition. | New York, NY : Routledge, 2022. | Series: Routledge focus on business and management | Includes bibliographical references and index.
Identifiers: LCCN 2022026170 | ISBN 9781032312217 (hardback) | ISBN 9781032312231 (paperback) | ISBN 9781003308652 (ebook)
Subjects: LCSH: Management--Study and teaching. | Industry 4.0. | Business schools. | Public-private sector cooperation.
Classification: LCC HD30.4 .D5 2022 | DDC 650.076--dc23/eng/20220815
LC record available at https://lccn.loc.gov/2022026170

ISBN: 978-1-032-31221-7 (hbk)
ISBN: 978-1-032-31223-1 (pbk)
ISBN: 978-1-003-30865-2 (ebk)

DOI: 10.4324/9781003308652

Typeset in Times New Roman
by MPS Limited, Dehradun

Contents

Table

Foreword

The pandemic has proved to be the ultimate test of our resilience, agility, and capacity to strategize and innovate in a highly uncertain environment. As painful as it was for humanity, the crisis has accelerated change in how work is performed and increased the need for versatility and fluidity of aptitudes and skills to help our organizations and our societies thrive.

This unprecedented context helped us to reframe the way we think about management education through the lens of lifelong learning, technology, collaboration, and the well-being of communities.

The global crisis also created an opportunity for reflection about our missions, values, purpose, and impact on society and the world we inhabit.

Even before the pandemic, we had witnessed the unbundling of education, with different shapes and forms coexisting rather than competing. This includes classroom-based vs. workplace education, mass vs. personalized programs, campus-based vs. online, structured vs. unstructured, taught vs. facilitated, and, increasingly, degree-based vs. skill-based.

In the increasingly complex learning ecosystem, established education providers like business schools and corporate universities compete and collaborate with emerging executive education players. Organizations can no longer afford to work in silos. They should leverage the ecosystem dynamics, which create a plethora of opportunities for experimentation and innovation.

Aside from competitive gains, global challenges such as deteriorating trust in democratic systems and social defragmentation urge all management development stakeholders to be part of a transformation ecosystem that includes the educational, corporate, and public sectors.

This very timely book, edited by three esteemed scholars and thought-leaders, Jordi Diaz, Daphne Halkias, and Paul W. Thurman, advocates for a partnership approach that will foster innovation in learning ecosystems. The collaborative ethos, exemplified in the book by several case studies, will not only respond to the ever-evolving workplace needs but also help establish cross-functional partnerships to tackle the world's grand challenges.

Prof. Eric Cornuel, President, EFMD Global

Introduction

Can Business Schools Pivot and Prepare for Training the Future Workforce?

In the post-COVID-19 era, business schools' executive education programs should guarantee agile employability for today's Fourth Industrial Revolution (4IR) business leaders, which can only be accomplished through their ongoing innovation of curriculum and teaching/learning methods (Crisp, 2019; Diaz & Halkias, 2021b). In reality, industry leaders and scholars label business schools as irrelevant executive education providers for today's labor market. Many business school graduates' scholar–practitioner gap makes the transition from graduate schoolwork arduous for employees and employers (Caporarello & Manzoni, 2020; Paullet et al., 2020).

Concurrently, the world is in the midst of the 4IR. The World Economic Forum named in 2016 the technological shift that is altering our very way of life daily and throughout all global regions. Economic, social, technological, and cultural changes challenge the labor market and consequently impact how business schools offer executive education to the future workforce (Caporarello & Manzoni, 2020). In this context, the triple helix hypothesis approaches the evolutionary linkages of universities, companies, and governments as inseparable and intricately linked hierarchical bodies rather than as independent functional domains (Chatzinikolaou & Vlados, 2019). The helix theory may offer beneficial explanations for the 4IR's upcoming activities, where "global hyperconnectivity" (Kelly, 2019) and computer programs will further inundate our everyday lives. However, technological advancement is not exogenous to the socioeconomic structure (Chatzinikolaou & Vlados, 2019). Only an evolutionary convergence of policy, technology, and management, which the different organizations should have the ability

DOI: 10.4324/9781003308652-1

to develop and collaborate on in partnership, will contribute to innovation in business schools.

Business schools can be relevant game-changers responsible for shaping economic and social change leaders. These institutions can respond to global and urgent social, economic, ethical, and environmental issues by teaching responsible management practices addressing the United Nations' Sustainable Development Goals (SDGs) (Diaz & Halkias, 2021b). The UN's 17 SDGs, 169 targets, and 232 indicators design a multi-stakeholder roadmap for global sustainable development, and they should be included in the business education programs' curricula as multidisciplinary core values and competencies for responsible management education (Falkenstein & Snelson-Powell, 2020; Laasch et al., 2020; Librizzi & Parkes, 2020). Specifically, business ethical attitudes and mindsets are significant in executive education programs since active professionals make decisions that affect the companies' stakeholders and society (Christie et al., 2003). Professionals are now called on to develop intrapersonal and interpersonal competencies related to sustainable management as part of their reskilling learning path (Orlović Lovren & Popović, 2018). Technological skills development is critical for professionals' reskilling, but executives should also be trained to contribute to grand challenges' global solutions, such as those identified by the SDGs (George et al., 2016).

Reskilling (learning new skills to do a different job) can help corporations to improve job security and ensure a more productive and stable work environment (Gagnidze, 2020a). Learning new skills to stay competitive in the job market is crucial to business sustainability, and many organizations are focused on supporting employee reskilling. Educational requirements for occupations expected to grow are generally higher than those for jobs displaced by automation (Agrawal et al., 2020). Incorporating *upskilling* (teaching and learning additional skills for one's present job) into business schools' executive education provides organizations and employees with an opportunity to stay relevant (Gratton, 2019). These economic, social, and labor shifts also challenge business schools' faculty to keep on top of their discipline, deliver state-of-the-art knowledge, and evolve professional development for their faculties (Halkias et al., 2020; Mlambo et al., 2020).

Today's most significant providers of executive education programs for reskilling/upskilling are business organizations outside the business school itself (Agrawal et al., 2020; Cukier, 2020; McKee & Gauch, 2020). The industry sector has usurped business schools' role as executive education providers due to academia's lack of readiness to transform curriculum designs for the future of work. Hancock et al. (2020) wrote

> *Many leading businesses realize that they cannot hire all the new skills they need. The better solution is to look internally and develop the talent they already have, as this approach is often quicker and more financially prudent and good for morale and the company's long-term attractiveness to potential recruits.* (p. 2)

How can business schools quickly pivot back to relevancy by providing reskilling and upskilling executive education that partners with industry to meet the changing workforce's employability skill gaps (Diaz & Halkias, 2021a)? The problem is that most of the approximately 16,000 business schools operating across the globe today lack the knowledge and preparation needed to forge business school–industry partnerships that provide short-term, uninterrupted digital learning opportunities geared to reskilling/upskilling a company's workforce (Gagnidze, 2020a; Morgan, 2020).

From a theoretical perspective, our work in this book is supported by a framework identified from concepts defined within the literature and grounded within disruptive innovation theory (Christensen et al., 2015). Markides (2006) and King and Baatartogtokh (2015) interpreted Christensen's (1992) original notion of "the innovator's dilemma," which eventually morphed into a theory of disruptive innovation (Christensen et al., 2015), by stating that disruptive innovation concepts are "new-to-the-world products" or "business model innovations" not just technological innovations. Disruptive innovation theory in terms of education consists of extending knowledge to allow academics to be the driver for creating improved access to high-quality education, designing personalized education, and circumnavigating the politics of education while deciding what needs to be taught and how (Arnett, 2014). This section presents a brief synthesis of knowledge and critical analysis of extant concepts grounded within disruptive innovation theory (Christensen et al., 2015) to formulate suggestions for an innovative executive education ecosystem model that reskills and upskills 4IR leaders to manage future changes in the workforce successfully.

Today's business schools must strategically work to redefine the concept of an *innovative business school ecosystem* through a commitment to experimentation and innovation (Halkias et al., 2020; Horn & Dunagan, 2018). This is a vision for a future where the business school becomes the disruptor to change the narrative about business education's impact on society (Carella, 2018). Business leaders must consider online technologies in education to educate future executives to transform the coming technological disruptions of 4IR into an avenue for world economic development and prosperity. Christensen et al. (2015) raised interesting questions as they debated their interpretation of disruptive innovation in higher education in *Harvard Business Review*:

> *The relative standing of higher-education institutions remains largely unchanged: With few exceptions, the top 20 are still the top 20, and the next 50 are still in that second tier, decade after decade. Because both incumbents and newcomers seemingly follow the same game plan, it is perhaps no surprise that incumbents can maintain their positions. What has been missing—until recently—is experimentation with new models that successfully appeal to today's non-consumers of higher education. The question now is whether there is a novel technology or business model that allows new entrants to move upmarket without emulating the incumbents' high costs—that is, to follow a disruptive path. The answer seems to be yes, and the enabling innovation is online learning, which is becoming broadly available. Real tuition for online courses is falling, and accessibility and quality are improving. Innovators are making inroads into the mainstream market at a stunning pace. Will online education disrupt the incumbents' model? And if so, when? In other words, will online education's trajectory of improvement intersect with the needs of the mainstream market? We've come to realize that the steepness of any disruptive trajectory is a function of how quickly the enabling technology improve.* (p. 11)

Three types of innovation need to be considered to understand the progress of business schools: sustaining innovation (not considered disruptive), low-end disruptive innovation, and new-market disruptive innovation (Christensen et al., 2015). Business schools have traditionally followed a sustaining innovation path, offering the right product better in the existing customer's eyes. Sustaining innovation typically favors industry incumbents and has three qualities: (i) it makes an already good product better, (ii) it targets the most profitable customers, and (iii) it improves profit margins (Christensen et al., 2015). Sustaining an innovation trajectory has increased the cost of education programs' operations due to their constant investment in research and student facilities and ultimately generating their programs' cost and complexity. Prestige and accreditation have served as the main entry barriers to innovation in business schools since both processes control operational strategies, attract customers, and offer business schools a long period of stability (Christensen et al., 2015).

This book is significant in advancing professional practice and promoting positive social change in line with the UN's SDGs to support sustainable business and community prosperity. This macro-level conceptualization is presented to answer essential questions and offer recommendations for practice, policy, and future research on how business schools' missions must become more aligned with global and labor economics. Business schools need to be significant social actors in transforming executive education programs by strategically engaging others in innovative education ecosystems through experimentation, innovation, and industry partnerships.

As academics and practitioners, our question remains: Where do business schools' executive education programs find themselves today, and how can business school leaders proceed successfully at a time of great transition not only in the workplace but through society at large? While technological skills development and workforce reskilling/upskilling can be accomplished, business leaders are most needed today to search for global solutions to today's grand challenges. Society is not asking for business leaders and managers who can "run the world" but for insightful, connected, and empowering agents who create positive social change in a volatile, ever-changing world (Diaz & Halkias, 2021a).

As one response to our question, this book culminates with a detailed applied case study defining how one group of academic and industry partners address the 17 SDGs through responsible executive education that teaches competencies most needed in the labor force. The second part of our book presents *The Bayer Active Leadership Program* developed by EADA Business School in Barcelona, Spain, in partnership with the Bayer Barcelona Corporation, and a second case study on various exemplar programs following the academic–industry partnership model. Throughout this final section of our book, we examine, through the lens of an innovative executive education ecosystem model, how concepts defined within disruptive innovation theory can be practically designed through robust business school–industry partnerships.

Part I

1 The Evolution and Devolution of Executive Education in Business Schools

Since the acceleration of the 4IR, the demand for education, economic development, and sustainable livelihoods has never been greater (Peters et al., 2018). The calls to action for business education to align its mission with managing the social and economic upheaval coming with the advent of artificial intelligence (AI) and technological innovation make business schools easy targets for disruption and innovation (Christensen & Eyring, 2011). Business schools find themselves at a crossroads between educating students to work in tomorrow's world and challenging the industries that support them to reform their missions (Halkias et al., 2020). Business school leaders are called on to reflect on how business education delivered to thousands of students daily can remain relevant in addressing challenges facing society and the business community and train them to reinvent themselves every three to five years (Çeviker-Çınar et al., 2017; Faix et al., 2020).

The evolution of business schools has been identified in three different periods (Currie et al., 2016; Kaplan, 2018). The first wave of business schools' expansion was connected to large and most multinational organizations' development and growth. Essentially, business schools were of critical support when leaders and management teams had to assume a high level of responsibilities relatively quickly (Khurana & Spender, 2012). The emphasis on business school activity focused on transferring managerial capabilities to this new professional who assumed a critical number of responsibilities (Kaplan, 2018).

The second period was when business schools became more research-oriented (Kaplan, 2015). Business schools' main concern became recognized and credited for transferring managerial skills and knowledge generation through academic research (Alajoutsijärvi et al., 2015). Faculty members' prestige and reputation started to be based more

DOI: 10.4324/9781003308652-3

on their research output than their teaching ability (Alajoutsijärvi et al., 2015; Thomas & Wilson, 2009). This era was also identified as prioritizing shareholder value (Dunne et al., 2008; Khurana & Spender, 2012). The two main forces guiding the second phase of business schools—research and capital value—generated technical managers' profiles with excess financial instruments and quantitative tools (Currie et al., 2010).

A third period coincides with a context of external pressures determined by globalization's complexity and technology development (Currie et al., 2016). Simultaneously, industry pressures led by the growth of international accreditations and international rankings generated a more process-based, suitable type of "reputation" for business schools (Dameron & Durand, 2013; Kaplan, 2018). This third wave required a more transversal research model and the inclusion of stakeholders in contrast with the previous phase focused primarily on shareholders (McKiernen & Wilson, 2014; Starkey, 2015). This shift coincided with different executive education providers' alternatives being introduced into the market, such as consulting firms and newly established, for-profit corporate universities, all with the explicit goal of addressing the growing need for skills development (Chen et al., 2019). Moving into the second decade of the 21st century, workers across industries must learn to adapt to rapidly changing conditions. Leaders must learn to match those workers to new roles and activities (Fung, 2020).

Business leaders are confronted with a new way of running their corporations for profitability and sustainability in the long term, accelerated by phenomena such as novel working methods, the COVID-19 crisis, and changing technologies (Hancock et al., 2020). To fulfill this acute demand for a skilled workforce aligned with market demands, small and large organizations in every industry have developed in-house executive education ecosystems (Hancock et al., 2020).

The replacement of jobs by machines has been a central tenant of the disruption in the labor market, driving the *reskilling/upskilling of the future workforce for the 4IR* concept (Diaz & Halkias, 2021b). The 4IR is characterized by the speed, scale, and changing role of machines and technologies in various business aspects while launching threats to existing organizations and innovating business models, strategies, and structures (Konina, 2021). Applying disruptive innovation theory to innovate business schools can only be done by responding to disruptive market phenomena (Christensen et al., 2015) and the need to reskill/upskill the future workforce after the COVID-19 pandemic. For the most part, business schools still promote and utilize a 20th-century executive education model on what and how they teach, how they are governed, and how to engage with their key stakeholders (Alexander, 2020; Kovoor-Misra, 2020). While education systems experienced a seismic shift during the COVID-19 pandemic, business school leaders have maintained learning systems from the last century limiting the experimentation and capability through innovation in executive education programs (Schlegelmilch, 2020).

For business schools to recapture the upskilling/reskilling provider role from in-house corporate programs more is needed than adjusting to automation, remote working, and AI. Stalled responses to a disruptive threat are often blamed on lacking understanding, poor executive attention, or insufficient financial funding. Little practice-based knowledge can be found in the extant scholarly literature on where business schools' executive education programs find themselves today and how to proceed successfully with developing academic–industry partnerships for in-house employees at a time of great transition in the workplace and through society at large (de Vries et al., 2020; Miotto et al., 2020; Trkman, 2019). Business school leaders are called on to remain relevant in addressing the future workforce and their employers and provide training for employees to renew skills every three to five years (Çeviker-Çınar et al., 2017). Can business school leaders recoup their role as premier business education providers from in-house corporate training programs through a market-relevant, sustainable, and digitally driven executive education ecosystem? This remains to be seen within the next few years.

A fourth wave in the business school development is recognized in parallel with the 4IR explosion (Kaplan, 2018). This new emerging era is when business schools will have to cope with their highly questioned credibility and legitimacy (Alajoutsijärvi et al., 2015; Collinson, 2017). Minocha et al. (2017) wrote that business schools must assume the enormous challenge of developing "imaginators, not managers." The response to the urgent need for reskilling and upskilling 4IR leaders will not be limited to business schools (Wigmore Alvarez, 2019). Nevertheless, more needs to be done when higher education fails to be an innovator, such as when a business school may find that it has not sufficiently planned for the future ahead (Christensen & Eyring, 2011). The networked business school itself can be seen as a disruptive innovation to further the student experience and aid the knowledge that a new generation of online business students can achieve through contemporary teaching approaches (Lorange, 2012).

Critics insist that after business schools unleashed their graduates to create a global financial crisis in the previous decade (Murcia et al., 2018), the time has now come for business schools to transform their learning models and broaden their students' training to address how the business community can meet economic, environmental, and social challenges for all populations worldwide (Nakavachara, 2020; Robinson, 2018). Such a transformation is slowly starting to gain momentum in business schools by reevaluating their role in reskilling/upskilling 4IR leaders to meet the demands of the 21st-century workforce. Business schools are called upon to reform their education models and approaches to teaching business and management skills, including the current graduate-level executive education paradigm (Scafuto et al., 2020; Shivakumar, 2020).

Executive Education

What is known today as "executive education" began in the United States (US) in 1945 with the first edition of the Advanced Management Program (AMP) at Harvard Business School (Amdam, 2016). The AMP was followed by two other *elite* executive programs offered by Columbia Business School and Northwestern University's Kellogg School of Management started in 1951. These senior management programs set the direction for modern executive education in the US and globally. Within the business school framework as an institution, a new sector of shorter, non-degree courses and programs was rooted (Moldoveanu & Narayandas, 2019).

By establishing the AMP, Harvard Business School crystallized two business schools as one institution (Moldoveanu & Narayandas, 2016). First, it was the two-year length of academic degree-granting programs at the master's degree level in the North American model; then, the other logic was based on shorter academic programs for practicing managers. The candidates' selection process for an MBA was based on grades and other formal requirements. In contrast, executive education programs were only based on candidates' previous positions and experiences within their organizations (Amdam, 2016). A few years later, the target market was much broader than the one defined in the original AMP. Middle managers, senior managers, and executives are considered the target market for executive education providers that differentiate their solutions into open enrollment and custom programs in the US and globally (David & Schaufelbuehl, 2015).

In the 1990s, companies started to consider executive education as an adequate catalyzer for organizational changes. The custom alternative of executive education—reported by the University Consortium for Executive Education—was responsible for 50% of business schools' executive education revenues through elaborated tailored programs. This shift coincided with different alternatives such as consulting firms, learning development organizations, and newborn corporate universities established by big corporations to solve the growing need for skills development (Chen et al., 2019). A vital issue for executive programs was that "the client" was the participant and the sponsoring company. The participants' motivation was mainly self-development, skill development, social development, and credentialing. Organizations invested in executive development enhance their staff's capabilities, improve coordination, signal commitment to a particular course of action, or create a new capability; they may be operating simultaneously with multiple motivations (Moldoveanu & Narayandas, 2016).

Business School Relevancy in the Post-COVID Era

The current fast pace of innovation has enabled the reinvention of entire industries in a few short years and even just months, rather than progressively over decades (Christensen et al., 2015). Estimates of the degree to which the economy will transform over the next 10–20 years include projections that by 2035 half of all current jobs will no longer exist, and about the same percentage of future jobs will be entirely new (Schwab, 2017). Disruption, scaled up from the employee's perspective to that of the employer, whether on account of the "gig" economy, big data and data analytics, value chain disaggregation, or even only due to innovation, is also imminent. Business-to-consumer industries, to which category business schools belong, will bear the greatest brunt, with industry slated to follow soon (Bradshaw, 2017; Peters et al., 2018).

A well-grounded concern is organizations' current demands to advance innovation and learning worldwide (Crisp, 2019). Scholars and thought leaders in education have concluded that business schools, as key providers of executives into the global marketplace through their programs, produce graduates who cannot, for the more significant part, be innovative in meeting today's global development challenges as outlined by the World Economic Forum (Barber, 2018). Technology has a remarkable impact on business, forcing changes to the hitherto accepted nature and notion of work and manager's role (Hill, 2018). Simultaneously, technology also produces uncertainty regarding the future character of jobs and the skills required to perform them (Sukovataia et al., 2020).

There is little consistent information in the scholarly or practitioner-based literature guiding business schools to develop an executive education ecosystem model that reskills/upskills 4IR leaders to successfully manage the future changing workforce (Caporarello & Manzoni, 2020; Fung, 2020). As the COVID-19 crisis has reshaped how work is done, the rapidly changing world demands have grown and accelerated, especially for executive education. Organizations are forced to ensure that leaders acquire new skills and knowledge and develop the new behavior and mindsets that companies need now more than ever (Caratozzolo et al., 2020). The opportunities identified in the literature resulting from this process are broad and do not offer a specific prescription for success (Diaz & Halkias, 2021b). It now remains in the hands of business school leaders. Developing these opportunities into a new business model for executive education is vital to educators and policymakers preparing for seizing upon existing megatrends to evolve regional economies in new directions (García-Feijoo et al., 2020).

Today, too many business school graduates are not equipped with employability skills resulting "from a lack of training on critical, integrative, interdisciplinary thinking, soft skills (social and personal), lack of attention to self-knowledge and reflective exploration, and a stronger focus on teaching than on learning" (Caporarello & Manzoni, 2020, p. 209). This outcome can be seen in how large and small corporations have taken it upon themselves to develop their own in-house executive education ecosystems to meet the pressing demand for a skilled workforce for today's market demands (Hancock et al., 2020). Business leaders find that the COVID-19 crisis, changing technologies, and novel working methods have pushed forward a new way of running their corporations for long-term sustainability and profitability.

Today's most relevant and utilized provider for executive education programs for reskilling/upskilling has appeared outside the business school (Agrawal et al., 2020; Cukier, 2020; McKee & Gauch, 2020). The industry sector has stepped in where business schools lack readiness and preparation for the future of work. In a recent McKinsey report, Hancock et al. (2020) wrote:

> *The pace and scale of technological disruption—with its risks of unemployment and growing income inequality—are as much a social and political challenge as a business one. Nonetheless, employers are best placed to be in the vanguard of change and make positive societal impact—for example, by upgrading the capabilities of their employees and equipping them with new skills. And employers*

themselves stand to reap the greatest benefit if they can successfully transform the workforce in this way. Many leading businesses are realizing that they cannot hire all the new skills they need. The better solution is to look internally and develop talent they already have, as this approach is often not only quicker and more financially prudent but also good for morale and the company's long-term attractiveness to potential recruits. (para. 4)

Nevertheless, a lack of academic readiness for business school graduates to properly prepare the present-day workforce for events such as a pandemic that disrupted job architecture across industries, and the skills employees need to survive in today's changing workforce requirements has called into question the relevancy of who is teaching the learners (Esposito et al., 2020). The ultimate challenge of business schools remains whether they can develop responsible leaders capable of navigating the increasingly complex economy and market society driven by the 4IR and post-COVID-19 work conditions (Agrawal et al., 2020; Ilori & Ajagunna, 2020).

Business schools play a critical role in advancing SDGs through higher education worldwide (Adendorff & Putzier, 2020; García-Feijoo et al., 2020). This macro-level conceptualization of innovative executive education ecosystems is presented through the findings of our research to answer essential questions of how business schools must be more relevant in global economics and sustainability and emerge as important social actors in transforming and updating executive education programs (Crisp, 2019; Setó-Pamies & Papaoikonomou, 2020). Business schools must consider a range of megatrends affecting today's business environment, the foremost being demographics, innovation, sustainable development, and technology, and how these trends will consistently alter the state of the global workforce (Fung, 2020; Morgan, 2020). To offer a new model of executive education and map the way forward for business school innovators, our work explores the issues of today's business school relevancy and concludes with suggestions for business school leaders for developing an executive education ecosystem with proposed areas of innovation that reskills and upskills 4IR leaders to successfully lead the future changing workforce.

2 The Reskilling Revolution and the Future Workforce

The Reskilling Revolution program launched by the World Economic Forum in January 2020 estimated that 1 billion people need to be provided with better education, new skills, and better work by 2030 (Schwab, 2017). Business schools must either take advantage of this opportunity to re-educate a growing group of market business leaders or become disrupted (Peters & Thomas, 2011). In response to a recent McKinsey (Capozzi et al., 2020) survey, 80% of 1,240 business leaders worldwide—up from 59% before the pandemic—said that capability building is extremely significant to their companies' long-term growth. The respondents also said that building the skills of existing employees is the most effective way to do it—far better than hiring externally, redeploying employees, or hiring contract workers.

Conceptualizing and subsequently testing new models for executive education programs within business schools is significant to academia and the business sector because today, there is both worker mobility and continuous change in building a skilled workforce (Moldoveanu & Narayandas, 2019; Paullet et al., 2020). This constant change in workforce skills is partly due to increased lifespans and changes in traditional working conditions, including shifting away from lifelong employment in favor of a diverse career portfolio (Fung, 2020; Painter-Morland & Slegers, 2018).

At the younger end of the workforce spectrum, individuals increasingly expect to be able to vary their career paths and, at the same time, continuously upgrade their skills in the use of new technologies. Organizations and business schools will have to design curricula that cater to the varying attitudes, values, needs, skills, expectations, and aspirations of multiple generations (Neal, 2017). The COVID-19 pandemic has intensified two trends: the need for new skills and competencies for employees at all levels, including digital skills; and the importance of upskilling initiatives to assist employed workers in

DOI: 10.4324/9781003308652-4

adjusting to evolving skill requirements on the job, as well as to prepare new job seekers for employment (Bergson-Shilcock, 2020).

Business leaders are requested to be the driving force behind this talent renewal, which includes social and emotional skills, adaptability, flexibility, and vital, digital, and cognitive capacities (Agrawal et al., 2020). People's work has changed drastically, and leaders are being challenged to do things differently at all levels (Capozzi et al., 2020). Most organizations struggle to generate the impact of reinforcing the essential skills for the future: leadership, resilience, and adaptability. Leaders prioritize self-paced learning and spend more time learning than before the pandemic. The combined effort made by both companies and leaders in reskilling themselves does not appear to be sufficient to cope with the challenges accelerated by the pandemic (Capozzi et al., 2020). A recent Gartner survey revealed that 80% of the workforce, 92% of managers, and 77% of senior leaders already felt poorly prepared for the future (Wiles, 2020). As the COVID-19 pandemic drives unprecedented market changes, neither the need for essential skills has ever been higher nor has the current workforce ever been less "fit for purpose" (Wiles, 2020).

The evident talent mismatch is a challenge for individuals and corporations in the Fourth Industrial Revolution (4IR) era (Dulin Salisbury, 2019). Five different categories have emerged to help individuals and organizations accelerate this transition—on-ramps, upskilling, reskilling, out-skilling, and education as a benefit (Dulin Salisbury, 2019). On-ramps—also known as internships—help companies to find and test difficult-to-recruit professionals, upskilling aims to keep the workforce relevant, reskilling retrains the workforce for new tasks, out-skilling supports existing employees to transition to new companies, and education as a benefit helps to recruit and retain talent (Dulin Salisbury, 2019). Employers claim that the need for skilled talent is so urgent that the conventional education system cannot keep up with demand (Liu & Murphy, 2020). Consequently, the higher education sector needs to transform the educational offering and what they teach and how they teach, promote current and new workers' success, and be sustainable (Liu & Murphy, 2020).

The proliferation of online learning platforms with broad accessibility to participants across the globe has contributed to a change in the way people gain information and new skills. Several factors, such as improved flexibility and cost savings, lead many large organizations and individuals to turn to online courses to gain new knowledge and enhance their management and business skills (Jack, 2021a).

The demand for online learning and training has only increased after the COVID-19 pandemic, which generated work-from-home mandates and limited travel between countries that substantially limited people's ability to enroll in residential, face-to-face programs (Huber et al., 2020). With on-campus initiatives, many universities and colleges are introducing hybrid or online learning and training that will likely impact how people learn (Dorn et al., 2020).

More than 3 million students studied entirely online in the United States before the COVID-19 pandemic—and 29% of all students enrolled in some form of graduate program were fully online students (Gallagher, 2019). According to the Center for Education and Talent Strategy, the majority (61%) of recruiting leaders consider online credits equivalent to or better than those completed in person (Gallagher, 2019). Instead of removing degrees, new forms of online credentials—various qualifications, MicroMasters, badges, and the like—play a complementary role, providing building blocks for more unique, affordable degree programs (Gallagher, 2019). Continued technological advancement in educational qualifications is increasing access to and supplying a wide variety of new opportunities for talent growth and corporate training. Furthermore, with a larger share of corporate learning now conducted online, the distinctions between institutional and on-the-job education will continue to blur (Gallagher, 2019; Horn, 2020; Jack, 2021b).

Amazon's "Upskilling 2025" and AT&T's "Workforce 2020" programs are just two examples of the massive efforts made by global companies to upskill and reskill their workforce. Amazon's initiative aimed at retraining 100,000 employees, or a third of their workforce, for higher-skilled jobs through 2025 (Morgan, 2020). The AT&T initiative included 140,000 employees who attempted to acquire skills for newly created roles (Donovan & Benko, 2016) as part of their new simplified organizational structure. Both programs indicate big corporations' priority towards reskilling and upskilling their tremendous labor force. Corporations collaborating with a complete executive education ecosystem that includes universities, educational platforms, and human resources (HR) internal training guidance are a perfect example of how corporations help eliminate skills shortages (Donovan & Benko, 2016; Morgan, 2020).

The adoption of technology has opened an opportunity for low-end disruptive innovation and new-market disruptive innovation to flourish in the business school industry (Christensen et al., 2015). The first innovation path occurs when new entrants provide new products or services to the low end of the market, causing incumbents to flee.

Three characteristics define this type of innovation: (i) it provides products that are "good enough," (ii) it targets "over-served" customers or those at the bottom of the market who require less product functionality, and (iii) it utilizes a low-cost business model. Following this path of disruptive innovation theory and accelerated by the exponential enhancement of technology, this value proposition—focused on affordability and simplicity at scale—has been able to not only attract the low-end segment of the market but also the one traditionally served by well-established business schools (Christensen et al., 2015; Horn & Staker, 2017).

Alternatively, new-market disruptive innovation offers the second option for disruption: turning non-business education students into students. This option (i) targets non-consumption customers who historically lacked the money or skills to buy and use the product, (ii) offers lower performance in "traditional" attributes but improved performance in new attributes—typically simplicity and convenience, and (iii) necessitates that the business model must make money at a lower price per unit sold (Christensen et al., 2015). Andy Grove described a strategic inflection point "as a time … of a business when its fundamentals are about to change" (McGrath, 2019, p. 1) in the business school arena. The pandemic has accelerated trends such as working and studying from home, offering the perfect conditions for both low-end and new-market disruptive innovations to happen and transform from an industry of two main educational stops (bachelor's degree and MBA) to a lifelong learning scenario with multiple and constant stops to be prepared for the 4IR accelerated world. Business school leaders must focus entirely on their business models, formats, and contents to offer solutions that genuinely cope with this enormous shift that will require an entirely new executive education ecosystem (Halkias et al., 2020).

Ifenthaler and Egloffstein (2020) defined the concept of *digital technology integration in learning systems* as a pool of critical knowledge to be studied by educational institutions seeking the skills and talent needed to conceptualize profound innovation. To initiate digital technology integration in learning systems requires specific patterns and connections of people in a changing institutional ecosystem. Kowch (2021) grounds Ifenthaler and Egloffstein's (2020) concept in complexity theory since a change in one part of the ecosystem can result in disproportionate changes elsewhere (Capra, 2002). Only when knowledgeable educators can lead schools and universities to adapt to digital innovation experiments can they genuinely transform their products and processes to be student-centric.

Applying disruptive innovation models to update business schools' delivery of executive education can only be done by developing effective responses to disruptive threats (Christensen et al., 2015). Addressing drivers and impediments in pivoting towards an innovative executive education ecosystem for reskilling/upskilling the future changing workforce may stimulate new ideas and suggestions that fulfill unmet social needs and create new social relationships and partnerships. In Table 2.1, a synthesis is presented of the critical arguments found in the latest business and scholarly literature about these drivers and impediments for business schools in reskilling and upskilling 4IR leaders.

From historical presumptions of stable, linear role-in-function structures (only dead systems are stable), educational ecosystems have shifted dramatically to dysfunctional systems with complex, interconnected elements where a shift in one part of the system influences all other parts (Hazy & Uhl-Bien, 2015). Practical guidelines are needed for innovation leaders who guide integrated solutions to transform and sustain a school or university with the right leadership team. For digital innovators and leaders involved in real change, classic approaches to leading and organizing limit the adaptive spaces required. Digital innovation teams have a better chance to adopt digital technology integration in learning systems and support in-depth impact on school and university change by forming competent relational teams to lead adaptive learning organization structures (Ifenthaler & Egloffstein, 2020; Thomas & Thomas, 2012).

The replacement of jobs by machines has been a central tenant in the reskilling/upskilling of the future workforce for the 4IR, but it is anticipated to quicken meaningfully in the coming 10–20 years (Liu, 2017). The 4IR is characterized by the speed, scale, and changing role of machines and technologies in various business aspects, exposing threats to existing organizations, and forcing modernization of business models, strategies, and structures (Konina, 2021). Indeed, automation may have a positive impact, for example, on ordinary high-volume process systems, where skilled workers are still expected to perform complex manual tasks and handle and control these processes and machines (Adendorff & Putzier, 2018). Although technological revolutions often fuel fears of decreasing employment opportunities as "robots do all the work," extreme automation, and robust connectivity, the 4IR's elements increase the productivity of existing jobs or generate demand for entirely new jobs (Halkias et al., 2020).

Business schools can be the pivotal platform for training business leaders to directly create economic and social opportunities throughout

Table 2.1 Synthesis of the key arguments about drivers and impediments for business schools in developing an innovative executive education ecosystem to reskill/upskill 4IR leaders

Rank	Catalysts for business schools to develop an innovative executive education ecosystem	Impediments for business schools developing an innovative executive education ecosystem
1	The reduction of the shelf life of skills to five years generates a lifelong learning market that forces business schools to re-organize their executive education structures from a one-time-only executive student to a repeat participant who has the potential to come back to be reskilled and upskilled. The urgency in workforce upskilling and reskilling will require fast content creation, delivery, and application.	Business schools have been slow to transform their learning models and broaden their students' training to address how the business community can meet economic, environmental, and social challenges for all populations worldwide. The traditional paradigm of business schools focusing on analytical models and reductionism is not well suited to handling the ambiguity and high rate of change facing many industries.
2	The 4IR will be about AI and technologies such as robotics, 3D printing, and biotechnology affecting almost every industry. Thanks to disruptive technologies, executive education will have the capacity to scale up personalized education to unknown levels.	Today's business education's mission is misaligned with managing the social and economic upheaval coming with the advent of AI and technological innovation that pervades business.
3	Companies will create their executive education programs with a multilateral group of providers, which opens a new role for business schools as potential certifiers of this company-led training initiative.	Education systems are changing, but many business school leaders have maintained learning techniques from the last century—this limits experimentation and the scalability possible through digital innovation in business schools.

(Continued)

Table 2.1 (Continued)

Rank	Catalysts for business schools to develop an innovative executive education ecosystem	Impediments for business schools developing an innovative executive education ecosystem
4	Meeting potential skills obsolescence will become a global challenge that will need a structural solution that will require a cross-functional partnership between different actors of the business education ecosystem. A partnership approach will move from a silo to a network approach where universities and other key players such as corporate universities, consulting firms, educational platforms, professional bodies, and professional certifications become part of the solution.	Given the speed of change and far-reaching impacts on the future of business, executive education leaders from academia today are challenged to an unparalleled point not just in educating tomorrow's leaders but for their very survival. Large student–faculty ratio, slow time to market of learning production, permanent academic teams, highly priced standardized programs, and the disintermediation of *professors to the company* will be the main challenges that executive education faces at business schools to respond to the growing need for a personalized, real-time, flexible, and scalable education path.
5	The UN 2030 Sustainable Development Agenda, as indicated in SDG 17, will require a *partnership approach* to achieve SDG 4 *quality of education*. A multi-stakeholder roadmap for global sustainable development will be included in business education curricula as multidisciplinary core values and responsible management education competencies.	This new era is considered the one in which business schools will have to cope with their highly questioned credibility and legitimacy.

6	Relational networks in education ecosystems can thrive with a reciprocal, shared (distributed) influence. Power is shared among these networks with high-capacity, decentralized teams that find autonomy and decision-making power during university innovation design and deployments.	Business school leaders need to focus entirely on their business models, formats, and contents to offer solutions that genuinely cope with this enormous shift that will require entirely new executive education ecosystems.
7	The speed of change has accelerated to levels requiring "real-time" education with hands-on application and a clear connection with the context of education.	Only when knowledgeable educators lead can schools and universities adapt to digital innovation experiments that can genuinely transform their products and processes to be student-centric. Business schools must rethink their added-value proposition to their customers—in terms of content and context—of their entire executive education to remain relevant in this high-speed world of change.
8	Post-COVID-19 outbreak will bring a "new" normal that will incorporate long-lasting implications in the modalities (e.g., face-to-face, online, hybrid) through which people learn. The spread of online learning platforms with broad accessibility to participants across the globe has contributed to a change in the way people gain information and new skills.	Practical guidelines are needed for innovation leaders who guide integrated solutions to transform and sustain a school or university with the right leadership team. For digital innovators and leaders involved in real change, classic approaches to leading and organizing limit the adaptive spaces required.
9	The Reskilling Revolution program launched by the World Economic Forum estimated that 1 billion people need to be provided with better education, new skills, and better work by 2030. Only a robust educational ecosystem will respond to such an unprecedented training need.	Delivering reskilling/upskilling educational programs presents many challenges for business schools. The rise of specialized and technical skills in the professional workforce requires constant upskilling and reskilling to keep pace with innovation within industry sectors. For the most part, business schools

(Continued)

Table 2.1 (Continued)

Rank	Catalysts for business schools to develop an innovative executive education ecosystem	Impediments for business schools developing an innovative executive education ecosystem
	The future of work will create more new jobs than those that will be destroyed. Reskilling professionals will be a standard business practice, offering business schools a new enormous pool of talent to be retrained for future positions.	still function through a 20th-century executive education ecosystem in what and how they teach, how they are governed, and how they engage their faculty and other key stakeholders.
10	Organizations do not know what jobs, skills, or mindsets they will need from the future workforce. Cooperation between academic institutions, businesses, and governments will be encouraged to anticipate and prepare to face this significant workforce transformation.	Leadership today is not what it will be five years into the future, and for the most part, related research has focused on business schools' role in reskilling and upskilling the workforce and is broad and scant, with little attention given to the state of executive education ecosystems in reskilling and upskilling 4IR business leaders.

their regions (Diaz & Halkias, 2021a). Delivering reskilling/upskilling educational programs presents many challenges for business schools. The rise of specialized and technical skills in the professional workforce requires constant upskilling and reskilling to keep pace with innovation within industry sectors. For the most part, business schools still function through a 20th-century executive education ecosystem in what and how they teach, how they are governed, and how they engage their faculty and other key stakeholders (Alexander, 2020; Caporarello & Manzoni, 2020; Kovoor-Misra, 2020).

3 Pivoting Towards an Innovative Executive Education Ecosystem in Business Schools

Leadership today is not what it will be five years into the future, and for the most part, related research has focused on business schools' role in reskilling and upskilling the workforce and is broad and scant, with little attention given to the state of executive education ecosystems in reskilling and upskilling Fourth Industrial Revolution (4IR) business leaders (Morgan, 2020).

> *In the future of work, the shelf life of skills is anticipated to decrease to five years, with individuals expected to update and refresh their skills six times throughout their 30-year careers to remain relevant at their workplace and employability will depend more heavily on lifelong learning and skills development, and less on initial qualification.* (Fung, 2020, p. 321)

The Business School and 4IR

Underlining this focus, business schools' capacity to change within the 4IR will govern their survival. To preserve their competitive edge, business schools must prove proficient in embracing a realm of disruptive innovation and either expose their structures to new levels of efficiency and transparency or face growing irrelevancy. Given the speed of change and far-reaching impacts on the future of business, executive education leaders from academia today are challenged to an unparalleled point not just in educating tomorrow's leaders but for their very survival (Edgecliffe-Johnson, 2019; Halkias et al., 2020).

Essentially, the 4IR has become the most transformative and disruptive innovation. The impact will continue to come from AI and technologies such as robotics, 3D printing, and biotechnology in almost every industry—from manufacturing and retail to healthcare and

DOI: 10.4324/9781003308652-5

entertainment—and have massive repercussions for the global economy and reskilling the future workforce (Halkias et al., 2020). Most business schools must support an ongoing process of upskilling and reskilling by forging into groundbreaking, disruptive innovation and rethinking their executive education ecosystem (Paullet et al., 2020). However, where business schools worldwide have failed to keep up with reskilling/upskilling professionals, corporations have stepped in to "usurp" the role of executive education (Gratton, 2019).

A study on accelerating skills in the age of intelligent technology was developed by Accenture and the G20 Young Entrepreneurs' Alliance (Accenture, 2019). Their results showed three significant areas that will require action from business schools. The first is to accelerate learning from experience; via the hands-on application, abilities are taught. The second is to shift the emphasis from organizations to citizens; organizations can expand their skills. Inside the company, they will cross-train employees on several specific skills. The third is to encourage vulnerable learners. It is important to recognize staff members vulnerable to technology changes and to be taught the required skills. This specific form of worker requires the most care yet is noted for fewer training opportunities (Paullet et al., 2020).

As vastly expressed in the literature, the required accelerated adaption and change found business schools in a 20th-century operating model far from the accelerated new business and education reality (Caporarello & Manzoni, 2020). A seed of hope is found in research on the most debated challenges for business schools, where it can be found the importance that innovation is gaining in front of all the other priorities found in the academic literature (Caporarello & Manzoni, 2020). As more businesses become "boundaryless" and national borders no longer define the rules of commerce, leaders of the future must find ways to become more engaged in "glocal" affairs—business practices that are global in nature but local in implementation (Halkias et al., 2020; Schlegelmilch, 2020). Specifically, scholars note that a gap in the extant management and business literature exists on how business schools can quickly pivot back to relevancy by providing reskilling and upskilling executive education that directly addresses 4IR leaders' evolving needs (Adendorff & Putzier, 2018; Miotto et al., 2020; Morgan, 2020).

Innovative Executive Education Ecosystem

In a 2020 McKinsey Global Survey, 87% of executives said they were experiencing skill gaps in the workforce. Still, fewer than half of the respondents had a clear sense of addressing the problem. The coronavirus pandemic has made the extensive skills gap in the workforce issue more prominent and in need of urgent attention (Agrawal et al., 2020). It remains to be seen soon whether hundreds of business schools worldwide can disrupt their present executive education model to an executive education ecosystem that can train business leaders and their managers to reskill and upskill their workforce in the post-pandemic era.

Morgan (2020) wrote that future leaders' primary challenge is to ensure new employees can adapt and existing employees can pivot to fill new roles.

> *We have always assumed that the things we have learned from our educational institutions and organizations would sustain us throughout our careers. Most organizations have no idea what jobs, skills, or mindsets they will need from a future workforce, so how can they train and hire for them.* (Morgan, 2020, p. 24)

Due to globalization, technology, demographics, the knowledge economy, and the need for environmental sustainability, business school graduates will need to manage more volatility more effectively, uncertainty, complexity, and ambiguity (the well-known volatility, uncertainty, complexity, and ambiguity (VUCA) phenomenon developed from Bennis and Nanus' (1985) strategic management theories) in the coming decade than in recent memory (LeBlanc, 2018). Today's VUCA phenomena dominating the networked world markets create the need and demand for MBA programs to train and graduate multiculturally skilled, globally intelligent, and adaptive managers (Millar et al., 2018).

"The traditional paradigm of business schools, with its strong focus on analytical models and reductionism, is not well suited to handle the ambiguity and high rate of change facing many industries today" (Schoemaker, as cited in Thomas & Cornuel, 2012, p. 330). Given the misalignment between the urgent need to educate businesspeople with business schools as the evident and precise response to solve this need, business school leaders are called on to reflect on the actual value and purpose of business schools' executive education programs to ensure their relevance (Caporarello & Manzoni, 2020; Paullet et al., 2020).

Large student–faculty ratios, slow time to market of learning production, permanent academic teams, highly priced standardized programs, and the disintermediation of *professors to the company* will be the main challenges that executive education faces at business schools to respond to the growing need for a personalized, real-time, flexible, and scalable education path (Moldoveanu & Narayandas, 2019). Future 4IR leaders will search for an executive education context where companies directly access business professors without their institutions' involvement (Diaz & Halkias, 2021a). Organizations in various industry sectors have already launched this initiative by designing and implementing their executive training programs with the accessibility to a growing market of new corporate learning players merged with independent trainers without having business schools and their slow bureaucracies as intermediary players (Horn, 2020).

More recently, executive education has become a rapidly transforming market, where certificates and digital badges have become a valuable option for almost half of the professional population (Huber et al., 2020). An increasing demand for high-level executive and managerial skills, coupled with the global trend of digitalization and 24/7 connectivity, may be heralding a new period of disruption for executive development programs (Moldoveanu & Narayandas, 2016). Literature shows that completing a higher education degree will not be sufficient for ensuring employability anymore (Ilori & Ajagunna, 2020), putting the upskilling and reskilling alternative for ongoing career advancement on the spot (Gleason, 2018).

Excelling in the 21st century's fast-changing workplace needs professionals to adapt to a wide range of circumstances, including different businesses and markets, varied positions and teams, and changing management strategies and business cultures (Diaz & Halkias, 2021a). The move towards lifelong learning will give business schools' executive education programs a chance to appeal to groups of consumers whom they have not yet served: junior managers who are looking to extend their set of skills and potential managers who are looking to be better positioned for the future (Shivakumar, 2020). With the growth of unicorn platforms such as Coursera, Udemy, Edex, and the so-called corporate universities and strategic consulting firms' role, the executive education market is too fragmented (Horn, 2020).

Distance learning programs, non-degree and executive education academies, as well as internal corporate "universities" are already making schools quickly rethink what "business" they are actually in (Halkias et al., 2020; Peters et al., 2018). Success at the organizational level increasingly calls for creative and flexible employees who can drive, shape, and lead change. Innovative executive education has a critical role in delivering such a workforce. To ensure its financial viability and stability, a school offering executive education must have sufficient numbers of students and clients willing to pay for it and be a part of what it ultimately produces for the labor market. Globally, there are some 13,000 business schools; and while many have attempted to offer reskilling/upskilling executive education courses, others have had to restructure or merge in their struggle to survive, while others have already closed their doors in the face of competition for training from the industry sector (Halkias et al., 2020).

Today, business school leaders' challenge is to recoup their role as premier business education providers from in-house corporate training programs through a market-relevant, sustainable, and digitally driven executive education ecosystem (Horn, 2020). Workers across industries must figure out how to adapt to rapidly changing conditions, and leaders must learn how to match those workers to new roles and activities (Fung, 2020).

The skills and innovations needed to gain a competitive advantage are continually evolving in today's economy (Caratozzolo et al., 2020). Improving staff efficiency is necessary for every organization and reskilling the current workforce becomes a requirement. AI can produce more jobs than it eliminates, according to Gartner (2017). Business schools and, more specifically, executive education providers will have to make corporate clients believe that business schools are offering "aspirin not vitamins," a must-have rather than nice-to-have solution (Jack, 2020, para. 12), in the words of Jean-François Manzoni, President of the International Institute for Management Development. The previous economic crisis—the financial crisis of 2008—saw a complete stop in executive education programs, while in contrast, the COVID-19 pandemic coincides with an acceleration of the 4IR that will not stop the retraining of leaders, whatever form it takes (Jack, 2021a). Business schools are responsible for training professionals and future leaders (Chen et al., 2019). They must collaborate to shape a more just and economically, environmentally, and socially sustainable world (Hambrick, 2005; Laasch & Gherardi, 2019).

4 An Innovative Executive Education Ecosystem for Reskilling/Upskilling Business Leaders

Educational institutions at all levels are essential for strengthening the economic development and global reputation of a nation (Gagnidze, 2020a). According to the digital era's changing needs, countries that have successfully transformed their educational systems can provide a digital workforce for private and public sector organizations. The digital talent shortage worldwide makes transformation necessary in educational institutions, especially in higher education systems (Cardenas-Navia & Fitzgerald, 2019). During the transformation process, innovative executive education ecosystems linking business schools and industry are much needed if business school leaders are to be key partners in reskilling and upskilling the future workforce in the face of the Fourth Industrial Revolution (4IR). Business schools must be willing to radically change their business model and integrate initiatives with industry with each one's elements embedded in the other through resources, people, and practices (Etzkowitz et al., 2021).

Although much has been written about the 4IR and its implications for the future of work, very little research analyzes the concrete solutions that can support the change needed to cope with such a transformational era (Rotatori et al., 2021). Rotatori et al.'s work shows four fundamental forces around the evolution of the workforce during the 4IR. The first one is an overall optimism around the future of work as more jobs are expected to be created than destroyed by the 4IR (Briggs & Buchholz, 2019; Manyika et al., 2017). The second one offers an emerging consensus about businesses taking the lead in the workforce's reskilling, bypassing governments and educational institutions' slow and inefficient response (Briggs & Buchholz, 2019; Friedman, 2016). The third force presents a sense of urgency to turn around academic institutions if they want to be part of a solution requiring up-to-date leaders for the 4IR (Hartley, 2017; Strauss, 2017). Furthermore, a final fourth force emerges together with the need to

DOI: 10.4324/9781003308652-6

reinforce a cross-sector approach to include not only businesses but also governments and academic institutions in the mission of serving society at large to overcome this significant endeavor of workforce constant reinvention (Brende, 2019; Ferreri, 2018; Rotatori et al., 2021; Schwab, 2017).

Today's companies work in a digital world that is volatile, unpredictable, and complex (Kraaijenbrink, 2018; van der Steege, 2017). The outbreak of the COVID-19 pandemic has worsened this condition. Organizations increasingly need a new generation of business and technology professionals who possess in-depth and up-to-date disciplinary specialization experience and connect and collaborate around the enterprise using business, innovation, leadership, and technology (Liu & Murphy, 2020). With rapid digital adoption by remote employees, company change has made intricacy and confusion the "new" normal (Wiles, 2020). A "new" normal that incorporates long-lasting implications on the modalities (e.g., face-to-face, online, hybrid) through which people learn (Li & Lalani 2020).

Combining the 4IR with the unprecedented times brought by the COVID-19 pandemic changes the way we live and work, changing the way business leaders are educated (Caporarello & Manzoni, 2020). Economic, social, technological, and cultural changes affect the labor market (Dyllick, 2015) and impact business schools' foundations. Education will no longer be the linear, one-degree equivalent to a work–life career but multidimensional with an ongoing upskilling and reskilling (Manuti et al., 2015). Business schools must rethink their added-value proposition to their customers—in terms of content and context—of their entire executive education ecosystem to remain relevant with this high-speed world of change (Diaz & Halkias, 2021a).

According to industries' changing needs, governments, and society, adapting business schools is crucial for filling the skill gaps and accelerating digital transformation across economic regions (Bughin & van Zeebroeck, 2017). Rapid digitization also brings uncertainty and complexity. In such a digital environment, the digital capability needs of companies change very fast. To support industries' digital skill gap, business schools must quickly introduce digital learning, development, and innovation to the center of executive education programs. In the digital age, universities are expected to have a structure that can manage this age by developing global and local strategies with public and private sector organizations (Aybek, 2017; Moules, 2021).

According to the results of the 2016/2017 Talent Shortage Survey conducted by ManpowerGroup, Japan (86%), Taiwan (73%), and Hong Kong (69%) are among those in the top ranks of high-tech manufacturing countries that have the most difficulty filling job roles. According to this report, a talent crisis emerges from two fundamental causes: lack of experience and technical insufficiency. The report emphasizes that the education system alone cannot develop the competencies required by the 4IR. At present, business schools have become inadequate to close this gap. What should be considered by business schools is how to manage tools and approaches for learning digital skills, how to make these processes more effective, and how to sustain lifelong learning (Cardenas-Navia & Fitzgerald, 2019). In this context, guidance and measurement assessment strategies should be followed, effectively monitoring, learning, and guiding the learners by employing digital technologies effectively (Aybek, 2017).

Business schools must be ready to provide a digital talent development environment using new applications that offer uninterrupted learning opportunities over traditional, blended, or multiple channels (Gagnidze, 2020b). Opening short-term training and certification programs to gain various professional digital competencies, supporting programs between industry, researchers, and students, increasing scientific research towards transforming information into reality, providing support for the opening of companies producing advanced technology within the university, establishing communication networks, and providing coordination between different subjects are other essential components of an academic environment aligned with digital talent development (Aybek, 2017).

In curriculum design, innovative and forward-looking educational policies are important for business schools to keep up with digital change, manage digital transformation, and train digital talents that meet the digital age's required competencies. Digital talent acquisition and internal upskilling of existing talents require effective partnerships between business schools and the industry (Diaz & Halkias, 2021a). An excellent example of such a collaborative effort is the Business-Higher Education Forum (BHEF). It comprises Fortune 500 C-level executives and leading university presidents dedicated to creating innovative education solutions and a highly skilled future workforce to increase America's competitiveness. A study from the BHEF and Burning Glass Technologies (Markow & Hughes, 2018) categorizes the digital economy's foundational skills into human skills, digital building blocks, and business enablers. Human skills are related to critical thinking, creativity, communication, analytical skills, collaboration, and relationship building.

Reskilling and upskilling programs require a three-step process that incorporates (i) identification of which skills are needed for coping with the new business reality of the organization, (ii) a clear recognition of the gap between the skills of today's workforce versus the new business model, and (iii) a selection of providers that will support the organization's reskilling and upskilling effort with the ambition of embracing in a lifelong learning journey (Agrawal et al., 2020; Brassey et al., 2019). The model is complemented by an easy-to-remember interpretation of scouting, shaping, and shifting to become a future-of-work talent accelerator organization (Hancock et al., 2020).

Project management, business process, communication data, and digital design are business enablers' skills that turn theoretical knowledge and skills into practice. According to one recent study (Markow & Hughes, 2018), a "blended digital professional" combines these three foundational digital skill areas with domain knowledge specific to a company, organization, or workforce, guiding business schools in developing an efficient and innovative executive education ecosystem. Promising partnerships that support the business school–industry cooperative business model with common goals have begun to be launched. The City University of New York and IBM partnership supports students in data science and analytics and urban sustainability. The Northeastern University, Raytheon, IBM, and Others partnership integrates work and learning in an industry-informed IT and cybersecurity curriculum, and the Washington University in St. Louis and Boeing partnership provides alternative engineering models for non-traditional students.

Digital talent management through reskilling/upskilling the global workforce in the face of the 4IR can translate organization-wide digital transformation investments into business success. Digital skills and capabilities need reskilling and upskilling of the worldwide workforce at all levels and operating on a continuously active learning loop. From the employee viewpoint, today's digital talents and experts value good work–life balance, learning and training opportunities, career development, good collegial relationships, and financial compensation, respectively (Diaz & Halkias, 2021b). Digital skills development is critical for professional reskilling, but executives should also be trained to contribute to grand challenges' global solutions, such as those identified by the UN's Sustainable Development Goals. PwC's partnership with UNICEF to help upskill millions of young people worldwide and Microsoft's global skills initiative to bring more digital skills to 25 million people worldwide are two examples aligned with the World Economic Forum Reskilling Revolution platform (World Economic Forum, 2020). These are significant numbers, but it will take many more initiatives of this scale and courage to address the growing issues of unemployment and inequality.

The challenge of business school leaders is to recoup their role as premier business education providers from in-house corporate training programs through a market-relevant, sustainable, and digitally driven executive education ecosystem (Horn, 2020). Workers across industries must figure out how to adapt to rapidly changing conditions, and 4IR leaders must learn how to match those workers to new roles and activities (Fung, 2020). Recapturing the upskilling/reskilling provider role from in-house corporate programs is about more than adjusting to automation, remote working, and AI. That is the tip of the iceberg. Today's 4IR leaders must have access to ever-evolving reskilling and upskilling training and education programs to support their workforce and deliver new business models in the post-pandemic era (Agrawal et al., 2020; Halkias et al., 2020). An example of an innovative executive education ecosystem in the making can be seen in Chapter 6 in our presentation of The Bayer Active Leadership Program in Partnership with EADA Business School.

5 Designing an Academic–Industry Partnership for Innovative Executive Education

The response to the urgent need for reskilling and upskilling Fourth Industrial Revolution (4IR) leaders has now jumped beyond the parameter of business schools (Diaz & Halkias, 2021b; Wigmore Alvarez, 2019). Introduced and defined by Deloitte as "a collaborative, transparent, technology-enabled, rapid-cycle way of doing business" (quoted in Sukovataia et al., 2020, p. 1783), the new term open talent economy generates an open market of providers for upskilling and reskilling. This critical change in recruitment behavior puts business schools and degree programs at risk since large companies such as Google, Apple, Starbucks, and IBM have changed from degree-based selection criteria to ones based on the candidate's skills and competencies (Sukovataia et al., 2020).

Engaging C-level business executives and business schools in co-operative partnership to shape the future of innovative executive education ecosystems is critical for guiding corporate and academic policy with shared goals (Dover et al., 2018). Their engagement can encourage others to build STEM and digital skills pathways for the future development of the workforce (Liu & Murphy, 2020). Building digital skills is critical for many intense jobs, including managing data, analyzing data, software development, computer programming, and digital security and privacy. Business enablers' skills have a synthesizing and integrative role in the workplace (Konina, 2021).

IE Business School in Spain (Center for the Governance of Change, 2021) analyzed 13 million job postings and over 500,000 syllabi from undergraduate degrees in three European countries. The IE Business School study focused on two main challenges for business schools: the need for more training in skills instead of focusing on non-skill-specific courses, and a better selection of the skills training that aligns with job market needs (EdSurge, 2016). IE Business School undertook this 2021

DOI: 10.4324/9781003308652-7

study to explore the need for a more skill-based curriculum in a business degree program, including further training for soft skills such as communication, teamwork, text analysis, and project management. More information is needed on a partnership between business schools and corporate partners to reskill and upskill business leaders effectively (Paullet et al., 2020).

Harvard Business School Publishing (Sawhney, 2021) discussed a new executive education program model post-COVD-19. The model presented for future-proof executive education programs pivots on these five characteristics: it is omnichannel, it is co-developed by business schools and corporate clients, it includes educational platforms as part of the delivery, it differs between low-cost online and high-end in-person options, and it focuses on skills building and credentialing rather than on knowledge transfer (Gallagher, 2019).

The role of higher education has been analyzed after interviewing 26 senior representatives from manufacturing companies in Ireland (Doherty & Stephens, 2021). Three main professional categories are identified: entry-level, competent, and expert, and by using a skills audit format, different skill development recommendations are made at each level. At the entry-level, senior managers emphasize the need for apprenticeship and upskilling in work-based learning environments to cope with the high-paced level of change in advanced manufacturing. A professional development program that focuses on cross-disciplinary manufacturing techniques and transferable skills is recommended at the competent level. Finally, at the expert level, short training programs that are action learning-based, incorporate best practices, and offer an intense residential format complemented with blended learning are suggested (Giesbers et al., 2021).

The pace of change in the manufacturing industry requires accelerated reskilling programs with faster, shorter bursts of work-based learning and experiential training are needed. With a growing demand for those at competent and expert levels, it is necessary to promote work-based learning to facilitate the upskilling of those employed in manufacturing roles, particularly in small and medium-sized enterprises. A university degree is still the most used credential to validate a candidate's capacity for a job (Pulsipher, 2020). A different approach to assess the skills of candidates would provide transparency, reduce disparities in labor market outcomes, and give employers better tools to understand the role of bias in their hiring and promotion processes (Diaz & Halkias, 2021b).

The pace at which the business world is changing requires an urgent and constant update in human talent. Skills learning has to be agile, able to adapt, and to align with changing business needs, and it cannot be exclusive for executives in the company but scaled to the entire organization (Suri & Hayes, 2020). Today, learners do not expect to receive learning when in class but whenever needed in an accurate "just in time" way. Companies must embrace a consumer attitude when planning their learning opportunities for their people. Companies are asked to generate an authentic "employer experience" for their customers.

As one of the world's leading telecom companies, the Etisalat Group has set out on a mission to deploy intelligent learning solutions for the skill gaps of today and the opportunities of tomorrow (Halkias, 2021). Through a combination of internal leadership training, an on-demand social learning platform, a specialist learning academy, and collaborative innovation formats, a "learner-centric" culture is being forged that aligns with an agile and digital world and supports Etisalat's mission and vision. Learning on the flow has to be incorporated into reinvented talent development programs that aspire to cope with the unprecedented, transformed business world (McKee & Gauch, 2020).

An example of an innovative executive education ecosystem is The Bayer Active Leadership Program in Partnership with EADA Business School. According to recent educational studies, higher education must enable students to improve "boundary-crossing competence," that is, in a transdisciplinary sense, the ability to effectively work, interact, and co-create knowledge (Giesbers et al., 2021). Actors from the various security-related networks (including higher education, technology institutes, and police academies) collaborated to create an MSc initiative to train security professionals and promote international security partnerships as part of a global network.

Like the envisioned MSc program itself, its design was situated in a blended setting, incorporated asynchronous and synchronous (online) communication, included cooperation in multidisciplinary teams within a community, and practiced boundary-crossing (Çeviker-Çınar et al., 2017). The new curriculum was developed by a multidisciplinary, geographically dispersed group of academic and industry experts. In conclusion, the design experience demonstrates that synchronous communication will greatly support transdisciplinary team-based instructional design in a blended environment. Optimal team-based blended instructional design, like optimal blended education, is all about striking the right balance between team members' ability to create context, introduce themselves to others, and be encouraged (Horn & Dunagan, 2018).

Part II

6 Case Study: The Bayer Active Leadership Program with EADA Business School

The skills and innovations needed to gain a competitive advantage are continually evolving in today's economy (Caratozzolo et al., 2020). Improving staff efficiency is necessary for every organization and reskilling the current workforce becomes a requirement. Meeting potential skills obsolescence will become a global challenge that will need a structural solution that will require a cross-functional partnership between different actors of the business education ecosystem. Such a partnership approach should aim at moving from a silo to a network approach where universities and other key players such as corporate universities, consulting firms, educational platforms, professional bodies, and professional certifications become part of the solution (Caratozzolo et al., 2020; Rotatori et al., 2021).

EADA Business School is an independent, non-profit higher education foundation created in Barcelona in 1957. Since its inception, EADA has been dedicated to the responsible training and professional development of managers and business leaders. As a non-profit foundation and an active member of its community, EADA is inspired by the principles of inclusion, sustainability, and transparency. EADA Business School has a unique history among business schools in Spain. Originally conceived as a family business, EADA had a particularly independent operating method. In a country where most business schools depended on religious organizations for funds and resources, EADA's success—or failure—was based on its capacity to generate revenue consistently.

As an ideologically and financially independent institution, its *raison d'être* and existence stem from the desire of a group of professionals to provide high-quality executive training. In the late 1950s, Ms. Irene Vázquez and Mr. Arturo Alsina initiated EADA's first activities as a consulting firm specializing in business education with a clear emphasis on the human side of management. The personality of Ms. Vázquez, a

DOI: 10.4324/9781003308652-9

doctoral graduate in industrial psychology, was present in all of the institution's activities—she insisted on incorporating the human factor into what was referred to as a post-Taylorism approach. As the years passed, EADA became a business school offering full-time master's, full-time MBAs, and part-time executive education programs for individuals and corporations.

In 2001 and 2003, respectively, EADA achieved the two main international accreditations, EQUIS (awarded by the European Foundation for Management Development) and AMBA (by the Association of MBAs), consolidating the internationalization process started in the 1990s. At approximately the same time, EADA began to appear regularly in the Financial Times Rankings for higher education institutions and individual programs. Today, EADA is constantly positioned among the best 50 business schools in the world (Cremonezi & Kwen Chan, 2020), and it is home to 1,000 open enrolment students from more than 60 different nationalities and 3,600 in-company training participants from 80 other corporate clients that year after year trust their personal development to the institution.

More recently, and aligned with the institution's strategy towards sustainability, EADA has achieved notable international recognition after being rated among the top nine business schools for their positive impact on society (Positive Impact Rating, 2020). The results of the student-voted Positive Impact Rating, a new global evaluation led by the Positive Impact Rating Association, based in Davos (Switzerland), which has the support of the UN Global Compact Switzerland, OXFAM International, and World Wildlife Fund, have consolidated the positioning of the institution as one of the best business schools in the world. Moreover, EADA is a signatory of the Principles for Responsible Management Education, or PRME, and a founding member of the Spanish Chapter of the UN Global Compact.

Because of the institution's origins in executive education, EADA has always had a particular sensibility towards this area and continues to place the corporation and its training needs at the center of its formative portfolio. EADA is considered a school for business professionals and believes this proximity to business provides a solid grasp of current management best practices incorporated in teaching and research. EADA's close connection with this corporate network is reflected in many corporate partners that entrust their training to EADA.

EADA has acquired a strong reputation as a quality provider of executive education in several areas over the last years. Historically, the development of management competencies has been EADA's key area of expertise in executive education. EADA can adapt its expertise to the different competency definitions the organizations use to design a training program to develop the competencies required to generate the expected change. The coaching methodologies applied help to transfer the competencies to the workplace. In the last few years, the institution has been developing its offer to include other new areas of expertise based on the research capacity of the faculty or through collaborative relationships.

EADA has always sought to deliver a "participant-centered" pedagogy, emphasizing the "learner." This change in emphasis calls for defining managers' profiles and the skills needed to perform efficiently in the company. Once these profiles have been determined, program-specific learning objectives are defined, the methodology chosen, and the system of evaluation decided. The learning approach is applied through suitable techniques for the programs' objectives, bearing in mind the participants' profiles. An active learning method emphasizes "learning by doing," giving weight to the process and the content. The mix of techniques stimulates participation and action, encourages exchanging ideas and critical thinking skills, improves self-confidence, and promotes feedback and self-evaluation.

The EADA brand is thus established as a solid and well-recognized brand in executive education at the local and national levels. Over the last years, a concerted effort has been made to position the executive education brand at the international level, competing with other schools and consultancy firms in tenders organized by multinational companies. As a true example of this strategy, EADA was selected by the German multinational pharmaceutical and life science company Bayer to jointly co-develop the Bayer Active Leadership Program for the Bayer Iberia market covering Spain and Portugal. Bayer, one of the largest pharmaceutical companies in the world, is positioning this leadership development program as a cornerstone of their newly established Bayer Iberia Talent 2020–2023.

Bayer Iberia Talent 2020–2023

The 2020–2023 reskilling plan has received the name "Bayer Active Leadership (BAL) Program" grounded in Bayer's Iberia Talent plan 2018–2021. While the former was focused on *assessing* Bayer's leadership team, BAL is about *delivering*, and it emphasizes generating a cultural environment where leaders can reach their full potential.

In recent years, the pharmaceutical and life sciences industry has entered a world of digital and scientific revolution in which the pace and magnitude of change are unprecedented. Constantly adjusting to a new environment is inevitable, creates challenges, and provides ample opportunities for growth for its people and the company as a whole. Bayer's unique vision, "Health for all, hunger for none," sets the foundation for our future and serves as the mark by which all activities across the company are measured. Bayer needs a perfectly prepared workforce to deliver on the business strategy and lead their respective markets to bring this vision to life. This will enable the company to shape them accordingly. Bayer will have to deliver world-class innovation, generate sustainable impact, and drive operational performance to accomplish this. BAL will clarify what is expected and needed from the company's leaders and employees to meet these needs in the current ever-changing world.

The BAL program is divided into three phases: *leading myself*, *leading teams*, and *leading business performance*. The first one is offered entirely by EADA's academic team, the second one is provided in conjunction between EADA's team and Bayer's Corporate HR team, and the last one is offered in partnership between EADA and Barcelona Data Institute, which is an external expert partner in data and business analytics that cooperates with EADA in all required programs. The e-learning academy complements the entire program Bayer has at the corporate level with three one-to-one sessions of coaching offered by EADA's external team of certified coaches. The program has to be followed by all 280 managers forming the Bayer Iberia team as part of the BAL Program for the Bayer Iberia 2020–2023 talent plan. It is organized into 10 groups of 28 participants to allow a strong sense of personalization. The total duration of the program is of six months, with a total of 180 hours between the time in class and out of class.

The BAL Program has a joint leadership team made up of Bayer's Iberia Talent Director, EADA's Corporate Manager, EADA's Academic Director, and EADA's Program Coordinator in charge of all administrative duties. For Bayer, EADA is the only "client" in charge of organizing all the different players participating in the program, ensuring program quality, satisfaction, and impact. The BAL Program includes in its design an Alumni Community facilitated by EADA's Alumni division that will serve as a lifelong learning community and is planned to be replicated in all the other 17 regions where Bayer operates on a global scale with a potential outreach of more than 3,000 future participants.

The Bayer–EADA partnership is an excellent example of how future-proof business schools can be part of the coined "reskilling revolution program" if they are willing to assume a new role as aggregators and facilitators of the imperative reskilling/upskilling workforce for the Fourth Industrial Revolution (4IR) leaders. Upskilling and reskilling touch so many unique needs that business schools are asked to assume a new role than they had in the 20th century. A strategic tension between the imperative need for reskilling and upskilling and, at the same time, the need for business schools to propose something different is present at business schools.

Business School–Industry Partnerships for Reskilling/Upskilling

The future of jobs will generate new jobs and destroy many existing ones. It is for the lower-end jobs where job transition will be more needed. To support this job transition, Beth Cobert—former US Chief Performance Officer—recommends that employers focus more on skills and less on credentials (Pacthod & Park, 2021). To make this change, company leaders should first define the skills that are relevant for any given job, look at their existing workforce to see if someone has the capabilities to assume this job, and finally make an intentional move towards incorporating a more diverse labor force supported by this new emphasis on skills rather than credentials (Longmore et al., 2018).

As reported in this case study, an example of such an innovative executive education program based on a business school–industry partnership is that of The Bayer Active Leadership Program in partnership with EADA Business School based in Barcelona, which is an integral development and reskilling /upskilling program for the 280 managers from the Bayer Iberia subsidiary. The program focuses on developing its organizational leaders' competencies to support Bayer's growth, complexity, and digital and sustainable transformation strategy accelerated by the COVID-19 pandemic.

Bayer was looking for a partner that could not only design, develop, and evaluate a leadership development program but a partner that could also incorporate internal expertise from the Bayer senior leadership team, internal asynchronous training from the Bayer e-learning Academy as well as the external input from a specialized training provider in data and business analytics. In a genuinely innovative executive education ecosystem, EADA has been able to act as a *connector* between all participating learning players by offering an upskilling and reskilling program that was coherent, consistent, and convincing for Bayer.

Executive education divisions at business schools need to build corporate programs under the frame of an entirely new business education ecosystem (Crisp, 2019). By grouping other universities and proactively incorporating a group of external stakeholders—such as internal company teams, e-learning academies, coaches, or specialized professional training centers—serving the imperative need for res-killing and upskilling in an integrative impactful learning experience, the participant is at the center.

Post-pandemic executive education programs will force institutions to prepare their teams for technology-based hybrid programs and identify and train their faculty to engage in online academic experiences and in physical face-to-face ones. Furthermore, business school leaders adapt their economic model for a new scenario. A higher up-front investment will be required and serve a market in which the attraction of digital-first future executive education students will reinvent the way business schools connect with their candidates. In an executive education market that the pandemic has disrupted, business schools are called on to renew their modalities and business models to succeed in a rapidly changing industry (Carella, 2018).

7 Reskilling and Upskilling: Selected Case Studies and Best Practices

A central hypothesis that has been proven in this text is that business schools can become if their leaders are focused and quickly innovative, training academies that can support significant portions of labor forces focused on credentials and skill-building. Indeed, this is a profound pivot—moving from degree-granting, relatively static curricula to innovative, ever-changing, certificate-awarding (and not just degree-granting) institutions. While the authors have provided several examples of ways business academies and their leadership teams are trying to pivot in these directions, the authors believe that it is even more important to describe both public and private successes where such pivots have been completed (and have continued to adapt to ever-changing market needs).

As such, in this chapter, the authors wish to describe situations where traditional academies and schools have successfully pivoted to upskilling- and reskilling-based institutions via a series of case studies. All information contained in these case studies is derived from publicly available sources, and the authors have no conflicts of interest with any of the institutions profiled. The authors hope that by showing how traditional academies and schools have either pivoted to upskilling institutions or have added such certificate and credentials programs to existing degree-based ones, the readers' institutions may similarly benefit from such innovative curricula and training offerings while simultaneously benefiting local labor markets.

Arizona State University and Thunderbird School of Global Management: Francis and Dionne Najafi 100 Million Learners Global Initiative

In January 2022, Thunderbird and Arizona State (ASU) announced the "100 Million Learners Global Initiative." The Thunderbird School

DOI: 10.4324/9781003308652-10

of Global Management plans to offer accredited online global management and entrepreneurship certificates through ASU. This program will comprise five courses in 40 different languages and will be available to learners worldwide. ASU anticipates that roughly 70% of the 100 million learners in this certificate program will be women and young women. Since this initiative is funded entirely through philanthropy, students who participate in this program will do so at no cost.

Recruitment for the 100 million learners program will be driven mainly by ASU/Thunderbird alumni worldwide. Global partnerships with public and private organizations will drive enrollment and feedback on initial course offerings. Google is helping to support translations of course modules into 40 languages by building a one-of-a-kind translation "factory." Philanthropic donations are being led by the Najafi family, with a $25 million seed gift, and ongoing operations are expected to be funded by alumni and corporate donors.

Students will receive a badge for each course completed. If a student completes all five courses, he/she will be awarded an accredited certificate that can be applied towards other educational/degree programs at ASU or that can be transferred for credit at other universities. Interest in this program is high, both in the United States and worldwide. This case example of a university and management training academy quickly pivoting to a five-badge model that can and will change over time in response to emerging market needs highlights the confluence of academic institutions blending with private capital and corporate partnerships to offer free, targeted education to labor markets that would otherwise go un- or under-served.

Telefonica's Innovation and Talent Hub

A terrific example of a corporate initiative aimed at both reskilling and upskilling its employees is evidenced by Telefonica's Innovation and Talent Hub. Telefonica announced in March of 2022 that it would build and open an entire campus dedicated to training workers. Its Universitas campus will be the heart of a "new learning innovation ecosystem" and "marks a milestone" in its learning history, says Telefonica's Chairman José María Álvarez-Pallete (Telefonica, 2022, para. 2). The vision of this hub, according to the chairman, is to consolidate the training value proposition of the Innovation and Talent Hub to expand its capabilities further and promote the most complete and powerful corporate learning ecosystem in the market.

The new campus is envisioned to have 2,000 square meters of space equipped with advanced technology and working spaces. Alongside the announcement of this hub, Telefonica also launched a "Power of Connections" program aimed at over 100,000 employees to inspire and connect them with the firm's purpose, vision, and culture. Specifically, the hub and connections program launch comes when education is emerging as a crucial requirement to enable Telefonica to respond to emerging digital challenges. Educational services and courses are available to any employee at no cost. While today's focus is on digital skill-building, offerings will change over time as market demands emerge.

Even better, Telefonica has also announced its foundation, Fundación Telefónica, joining the hub's strategy to boost employability and remove barriers that make access to digital education possible for the most vulnerable. In this way, Telefonica will help boost the productivity and skillsets of its employees and make digital education more accessible and available to potential labor markets outside the firm.

Wawiwa Tech (Wawiwa)

Nevertheless, what kinds of firms can provide such upskilling and reskilling that firms like Telefonica need? Do firms need to build these capabilities or "internal universities" themselves, or can they outsource these needs and be confident that a partner—either a private–private partnership or public–private one—will not only train the skills needed today but also be able to anticipate changes in training needs for the future?

In Israel, Wawiwa Tech (Wawiwa) purports to provide technology-focused skills training efficiently and flexibly to meet today's needs and educate workforces for future needs. Wawiwa points to Microsoft, Google, and IBM efforts to reskill and upskill "millions" for technology and how they can help make such giant leaps a reality. They point to the commonly stated statistic that by 2030 a shortage of technology workers could approach 85 million. Thus, Wawiwa is focused solely on technology skill-building and upskilling, nothing else.

Nevertheless, why only technology skills? Part of the answer is that this is Wawiwa's "DNA"—they were borne out of technologist founders who were in need of quick technology upskilling. The other part is that Wawiwa happens to live in one of the most technologically innovative economies in the world: Israel. Often referred to as the "Startup Nation," Israel has deep innovation, startup, and technology roots from its technology universities, commercial partnerships with other technology leaders, and relatively low-cost application and system development infrastructures. In short, if someone wants to build something quickly to prove a concept and then scale it when a market is ready, technology development in Israel is a reasonably good bet.

Also, Israel is always focused on training new labor audiences either inside the country (e.g., Orthodox Jews entering the workforce, soldiers completing compulsory military service in the Israeli Defense Forces, technology-focused K-12 curricula) or outside (e.g., partnerships with the UK government to support the UK National Skills Fund). Thus, Israelis are well trained in technology from an early age, and the country has effectively repurposed these training models to serve the interests of firms that need technology upskilling and reskilling for their workforces.

Thus, Wawiwa is an excellent example of a private firm with government backing that has a laser focus on specific skills training for (large) employee populations.

Skilled Education

Skilled Education is another example of a public–private partnership in the upskilling space that brings together government, industry, and academia. Skilled Education, an online education provider in the United Kingdom, has been appointed by the UK government to develop a flagship upskilling program to support small businesses. The UK government's "Help to Grow: Management" post-pandemic initiative aims to upskill over 30,000 business leaders with the help of Skilled Education over three years.

Skilled Education designs and delivers online learning pathways, "microcredentials," and degrees, and they have a successful history of working with partners such as the University of Cambridge, London School of Economics, and UWE Bristol. Like so many companies and training academies, Skilled Education believes that COVID-19 has accelerated changes in how we work, learn, and live. While most agreements between private firms and governments focus on policy and regulation, the agreement between Skilled Education and the UK government includes program design.

Furthermore, while this model may seem relatively new post-COVID-19, it has worked successfully for other training academies. Coursera and UpGrad, for example, have outstanding track records as international education companies that help governments with upskilling and training needs. Skilled Education expects the programs it designs in conjunction with the UK government to be delivered by over 50 UK business schools alone.

Nevertheless, helping schools is not the only sector on which Skilled Education focuses. Helping small and medium-sized enterprises recover from COVID-19 impacts is critical to the labor market, and enterprise success since COVID-19 has accelerated the need for skills training in specific areas without requiring degrees. The Help to Grow program expects to utilize a 12-module program to help business owners and leaders develop solid growth plans for their firms. Focusing on markets beyond the UK border is also part of the developed instruction. As it stands now, any CEO or senior team member of a UK business employing between 5 and 249 people is eligible for the program.

Range: Professional Development for the Modern Workforce

A startup incubated in Columbia University's "Columbia Entrepreneurship" initiative, Range purports to provide upskilling programs to companies so their workforces can gain skills and competencies to become "overachievers." Range has a simple mission: to empower others. Range believes that diversity and inclusion should apply to the workforce members and their skills and competencies. By providing employees with the tools necessary to develop continually, Range seeks to upskill employees and inspire them to maximize their potential.

Range essentially acts as a consolidation platform for other turnkey skill-building services such as Udacity, MasterClass, Pluralsight, Coursera, and Udemy. Thus, as a platform provider, Range can help to provide employees with company-approved skills training and track the performance of that training over time. Range is, in essence, an outsourced professional development provider. This allows managers to focus more on business and less on professional development management, permits all employees to be engaged at their individual paces, provides analytics so managers can assess skill development and competence achievement, and offers a single platform from which any professional development interaction can be had. Therefore, employees will effectively "own" their growth, pick different skills to build so they do not become "pigeonholed" over time, and manage their skills building—and, by extension, their career growth—via a single, easy-to-use platform.

As more providers of online skill-building content emerge, more firms are emerging to consolidate/handle the multiple training touchpoints often encountered by firm management (especially professional development) and employees who want to find ways to meet job performance evaluation gaps through focused training. Therefore, it should be no surprise that university incubators, like the one founded by Columbia University's president, are creating more firms like Range to provide "portal" solutions for employees and employers.

Reskilling China: Transforming the World's Largest Workforce into Lifelong Learners

The subtitle above not only represents an unprecedented economic and educational challenge but is also the title of a research report (Woetzel et al., 2021) by McKinsey & Company in January 2021. After three decades of reformation in its educational system, China has created a workforce geared for an industrial economy. Nevertheless, the digital economy abounds now, and according to the authors, up to a third of global occupational and skill transitions may occur inside China. For example, by 2030, some estimate that 30%—or 220 million Chinese workers—may need to transition occupations due to automation. This will require a massive—and quick—transformation of China's skills training infrastructure, specifically with a move towards digital transformation, to retool its workforce for the Fourth Industrial Revolution.

The report goes on to postulate that several key "levers" will be essential for this transformation, including the adoption of digital technologies, fostering of "collaboratives" between education companies and the government, creation of vocational "tracks," and creation of incentives such as microcredentials. As both occupations and skills "transition" to new (digital-driven) models, fundamental changes in how existing workers are upskilled and reskilled will be necessary. Creating vocational tracks implies that many new workers will not necessarily go through degree-based education but vocational-based skill-building. Thus, a new educational and training system for Chinese workers will have to serve more of them, with more skills training, in more digital (non-classroom-based) ways.

This last requirement—training ubiquity—will be one of the most challenging for China but also, perhaps, one of the more opportunity-rich ones for firms with training and upskilling platforms catered to the Chinese labor force (and its "vocational tracks"). China already has some such online platforms and systems, but they need to be scaled to the workforce—and skill needs—of the future. For example, DHL, the global shipping and logistics company, cites much of the McKinsey report in its own "globalization" priorities and is actively seeking to address precisely these needs in all markets in which it operates.

Guild: Doing Well by Doing Good

Many upskilling and reskilling services, digital and otherwise, tend to focus on "white collar" workers—i.e., those with a college degree—who primarily work in non-hourly paid jobs (or the so-called salaried employees). Based in Denver, Colorado, Guild is also focusing its efforts on the "blue-collar," or unskilled workforce ... much of which is often displaced by digital transformation, automation, or corporate consolidation. Guild purports to bridge the gap between education and employment (in the United States) by partnering with America's largest employers to build education and reskilling experiences for their employees. Similar to Range and others already profiled, they do this by connecting employees to a marketplace of universities and training academies focused on working adults.

The Guild system allows employers to pay for upskilling/reskilling courses up-front so workers can focus on their coursework and skill-building. Workers have access to additional educational and career services with personalized support if needed. Since Guild exists as a public benefit corporation (essentially a not-for-profit), it only does well if its customers (learners and firms) do well. This model is quite novel in the reskilling/upskilling provider space since Guild focuses on building communities from the ground up and then helping those communities succeed. By sitting at the intersections of workers, employers, and learning providers, Guild can truly customize different "communities" to benefit its market participants. As such, not only do learning providers get access to a broader, more diverse audience, but employers enjoy up-to-date skill-building offerings and communities that can be customized to fit learner/employee needs.

For example, in March 2022, PepsiCo joined the Guild family. PepsiCo offers more than 100,000 frontline and professional employees (US-based) a debt-free college degree program through Guild. This program, which is expected to have smaller, non-degree upskilling offerings in the future, will cover 100% of tuition costs, books, and fees. Other US-based companies such as Kohl's and Hilton Hotels have joined Guild to create similar programs.

Ernst and Young Tech MBA: Managed by Hult International Business School

A different kind of graduate degree program for working professionals seeking to upskill their business acumen is now available for Ernst and Young (EY) employees and is offered through the Hult International

Business School (Hult). Formerly known as the Arthur D. Little School of Management in Cambridge, Massachusetts, Hult is now a global business school offering undergraduate and graduate degree programs, with campuses in Cambridge (US), London (UK), San Francisco (US), Dubai (United Arab Emirates), Shanghai (China), New York City (US), and Ashridge (UK). Hult also provides distance learning programs—degree and non-degree—to students in Australia, New Zealand, and many countries in Africa. Hult's global reach has only increased through the development of such "corporate" degree programs.

In July 2020, EY and Hult announced the first-ever "corporate MBA," which is free to any of EY's 300,000 employees, regardless of rank or location (150 countries), and can be finished in any duration. Curricula are updated every four months. The program consists of online learning, practical experiences, insight papers, and a capstone project. This is a notable example of an employer partnering with a school to create its own outsourced "university" (compared to other firms that try to build such capabilities internally or use "portal" solutions, like those mentioned earlier, to connect employees to learning content).

Even though the EY Tech MBA is solely a master's degree program with some student customization allowed, this program builds upon the "EY Badges" program through which employees earn digital credentials in future-focused skills by learning and applying their new skills in practice. In fact, to obtain the EY Tech MBA degree, an employee must complete or earn 16 badges spanning the domains of leadership, technology, and business topics, as well as three-pillar papers and a capstone project. As of February 2021, EY reports that over 100,000 badges have been awarded to EY employees.

Thus, this corporate MBA gives us an example of how an employer can create credentials or "badges" program that can be used to both build specific, targeted skills and allow growth through attainment of an accredited master" degree in business administration if that is an employee's goal.

Industry–Institution Partnerships for Improved Labor Market Upskilling: Malaysia

We pivot now to look at the role of government and how it can successfully—and unsuccessfully—create stimuli in regional economies to promote upskilling and reskilling of significant portions of its labor force. In mid-2020, economists in Malaysia studied the impact of industry-driven technical and vocational education and training. They aimed to determine the best ways to create industry–institution partnerships to foster upskilling and reskilling and hypothesize the best business sector and government policies to support such partnerships.

In the early 1990s, as the Industrial Revolution swept through Asia, industries were compelled to produce highly skilled workforces to promote knowledge-based skills in several commercial sectors in Malaysia. The Malaysian government initiated the Technical Vocational and Education and Training (TVET) program in anticipation of these labor market effects. This program was heavily pedagogy-based and driven by national universities/schools (and thus via degree attainment). However, 20+ years later, economists agree that the TVET program did not reach its full potential mainly because pedagogy was controlled more by the education "suppliers"—schools, universities, and government policy—and not enough by the skill "demanders" in the market—employers and business partners.

However, the model in and of itself does have merit, the researchers argued, if it could become more demand-driven. That is, if the employers and firms themselves could partner with the schools and training academies, perhaps this model would create not only faster paths to upskilled laborers but also more agile curricula that could "flex" over time as labor market skills need to be changed. Thus, through a variety of qualitative and survey data, the researchers were able to conclude that such an industry–institution partnership model could work more effectively if several preconditions—i.e., government policies—were put in place.

First, companies should be able to freely partner with academic institutions to provide an environment of empowerment and "lifelong learning" for their employees. Second, academic institutions, even those run by the government, should be able to scale up in order to effectively deliver such upskilling/reskilling training programs. Third, private sector interests—training academies, vocational schools, etc.—should also be allowed access to these upskilling "markets" to provide innovative solutions to lifelong learning needs/demands in the market.

According to the research, results from this study have been put forth to the Malaysian government as part of its "Education Blueprints 2013–2025" efforts. Regardless of the outcome, however, it is of interest to see how the level of government intervention in (educational) program design can affect outcomes in the present tense and also for years to come. Given that the focus here is on worker skill enrichment, there is some validity to the argument here that a more "free market" approach to innovation and partnerships in lifelong learning may be at least as effective as a centralized/government policy-driven agenda.

Note that similar results of economic studies in southeast Asia, Australia, South Africa, Kenya, Saudi Arabia, and the United Arab Emirates confirm many hypotheses proffered in the Malaysian work.

Conclusion

As shown above, filling skill gaps for employees—with or without formal educational backgrounds—is a difficult problem to solve. However, it is not because training them is difficult. The challenge is aligning market demand with employee desire in a flexible curriculum that can be easily changed over time in a government/policy structure that supports multiple partnerships to deliver an upskilled workforce.

However, more governments and academies are realizing that only public–private and private–private partnerships can help solve the upskilling conundrum. With this in occurrence, surely more labor forces—large and small, government and private—can realize value from the multitude of lifelong learning and upskilling platforms, content, and management tools available today, some of which have been highlighted above.

8 Thoughts and Notes for Business School and Management Education Leaders: Where Do We Go from Here?

More research is needed to help education systems recognize tensions, establish new purposes, and mitigate formal epistemologies in the context of digitization (Kowch, 2021). Research is necessary to identify the attractors that engage innovative educators in a team and the ecosystem-level resource problems. Education systems are changing—but many business school leaders have maintained learning systems from the last century—this limits experimentation and the scalability possible through digital innovation in business schools (Schlegelmilch, 2020). Disruptive innovation theory can be further applied in understanding and making recommendations for building innovative business school programs on data from relevant research questions addressing today's global marketplace challenges such as gender-related issues and digital entrepreneurship, AI, technology diffusion in developing economies, and the impact of business on economic development and sustainability (Diaz & Halkias, 2021b; Dover et al., 2018). As the COVID-19 crisis has reshaped how work is done, the rapidly changing world demands have grown and accelerated, especially for executive education. Organizations are forced to ensure that leaders acquire new skills and knowledge and develop the new behavior and mindsets the companies need now more than ever (Caratozzolo et al., 2020).

Business schools must accelerate their pace of innovation in reskilling and upskilling executive boardrooms to map a new road that points the way to new measures of progress and is consistent with the new generation's values in preparing to lead (Samuelson, 2021). Designing innovative executive education ecosystems must focus on how business schools can become more relevant in global economics and sustainability and emerge as important social actors in transforming and updating executive education programs to address their skilling/upskilling gap in the future workforce (Crisp, 2019; Setó-Pamies & Papaoikonomou, 2020).

DOI: 10.4324/9781003308652-11

Digital talent development for business schools is crucial for preparing skilled graduates for the digitally dominated business environments and strengthening regional economic development (Karaboga et al., 2021). The importance of collaboration between businesses, schools, and industry to create a digital talent ecosystem cannot be overstated when addressing the global digital talent gap. Partnerships between business schools and industry provide opportunities to assist students, researchers, managers, entrepreneurs, and policymakers for sustainable talent development by giving them a chance to discover, support, and bring in potential digital talents across regional economies. The common goal of business school–industry collaboration is to develop a strong bond among the partners for knowledge, technology, and organizational transfer to support digital skills development (Diaz & Halkias, 2021a). Developing both global and local strategies with the cooperation of business schools and regional industries can offer a vision of a future-focused workforce through careful consideration of five inter-related elements.

Thriving in the Digital-First Future Will Require New Capabilities

The chairman of a large financial services company recently reported that he views his firm as a technology company that operates in the financial services industry. Awareness of technology has become critical in today's technology-driven business world. Moreover, with tremendous data abundance due to technological advancements and evidence-based decision-making, data literacy is also essential. So, any professional ready for this world needs to possess the technology and data-based literacies enhanced by human-centric capabilities such as collaboration, creativity, and entrepreneurial and systems thinking as critical determinants of future success. Without these "human skills," individuals cannot utilize their technical skills to their full potential. Furthermore, part of the importance of these foundational skills is that, unlike technical skills, which often have a short shelf life, they are valuable throughout a lifetime of work. Executive development programs have to aspire to do just that: find the right mix of digital and human skills to develop future leaders.

Shaping Real-Time Business Capabilities Are Made Possible Through Learning in Workflow

In tandem with the COVID-19 recession, automation creates a "double-disruption" scenario for workers. In addition to the current disruption from the pandemic-induced lockdowns and economic contraction, companies' technological adoption will transform tasks, jobs, and skills by 2025. Integrating academic lessons with con-textualized experiential learning projects as part of everyday work shapes learning skills in real-time and for immediate use. In future-ready programs, participants must demonstrate the application of academic concepts in their projects as a required component of each course. In other words, the return on investment is immediate for both companies and their employees. Also, participant projects are not one-size-fits-all projects; they choose projects of interest. This personalized learning is bound to pay dividends for corporate partners. Besides, given the content development's unbundled nature, these learners can also receive university credit during the upskilling process, broadening the talent pool with cutting-edge capabilities and credentials.

Co-creating with Industry Partners is Critical for Success

The future of work is changing rapidly, and agility is essential to serve business school corporate allies' talent needs. The necessary founda-tion for building a digital-first, diverse workforce can only be con-structed efficiently if academic institutions and industry work together towards a common goal. By co-creating and co-building educational offerings with industry partners, companies and universities can combine their strengths towards developing impactful leaders. Business schools are uniquely suited for all of this work. They have been pioneers in experiential education for over a century, and fusing academic rigor with real-world relevance is what they do best.

Executive education leaders and faculty at business schools have always viewed the industry allies as their "faculty in the field," so these collaborations come naturally to them. Business schools work with corporate allies, which has enabled them to respond to their needs and develop impactful academic content accordingly. This has also enabled them to further develop the future of contextualized learning to fa-cilitate metacognition for their learners. There is a clear potential for embracing "revolutionary" collaborations, which will open the door to new possibilities.

Co-creating with Alternative Education Providers Will Accelerate the Response

Business schools will have to transition from a fixed mentality of a one-stop learning place to a flexible one. Executive education participants will be part of a continuous journey that will require different elements to cope with Fourth Industrial Revolution (4IR) challenges. Business schools' only way to respond in form and speed to the massive need for upskilling and reskilling will require coordination between different learning providers. They will need to include new corporate learning players to offer complex programs that incorporate hard skills, soft skills, and digital skills in real-time and at scale. The "new" normal will be about content as the delivery model in the executive education experience.

The combination of traditional academic providers (i.e., business schools) with online delivery mode experts (i.e., platforms) will be complex, and it will require flexibility from both parties, always with the participation of recipient organizations. Business schools will need to assume a different role in which they genuinely co-create with businesses and educational alternatives that fit the need in real-time. The variety of time and place combinations will require highly competent and motivated business school leaders committed to making this work. It will require a degree of intentionality that is unnecessary for traditional academic practices. For academic leaders, that means being empathic and listening to corporate needs while also developing solutions.

"The traditional paradigm of business schools, with its strong focus on analytical models and reductionism, is not well suited to handle the ambiguity and high rate of change facing many industries today" (Schoemaker, as cited in Thomas & Cornuel, 2012, p. 330). The key challenges that executive education faces at business schools as they attempt to respond to the growing need for flexible, real-time, personalized, and scalable education paths include the disintermediation of *professor to company*, slow time to market of learning production, large student–faculty ratio, high-priced standardized programs, and permanent academic teams (Moldoveanu & Narayandas, 2019). There is a misalignment between the pressing need to educate businesspeople and business schools as the precise and evident response to this need; the leaders of business schools are thus compelled to reflect upon the actual purpose and value of business schools' executive education programs if they are to ensure their relevance (Caporarello & Manzoni, 2020; Paullet et al., 2020).

When planning their curriculum, opening short-term training and certification programs to gain various professional digital competencies has been an afterthought for most business school leaders. Additionally, academics in business schools must be willing to let go of their "exclusive knowledge ownership" of the executive education learning process and take an equitable role with industry partners in designing and developing innovative executive education ecosystems. A new age of disruption in executive development may be in the making, as indicated by the global trends of digitalization and 24/7 connectivity and the growing demand for high-level managerial and executive skills (Moldoveanu & Narayandas, 2016).

While many of the roughly 16,000 business schools in the world have tried to offer reskilling/upskilling executive education courses, some have already shut down in the face of competition from the industry sector concerning training, and others have had to survive by merging or restructuring (Halkias et al., 2020). A business school's executive education programs need to have many clients and students who want to give money for it and have a place in what it generates for the labor market, ultimately ensuring its financial stability and viability. However, research indicates that employability is no longer sufficiently assured by completing a higher education degree (Ilori & Ajagunna, 2020); this puts the reskilling and upskilling alternative for continuous career advancement on the spot (Gleason, 2018).

The Bayer Active Leadership Program in partnership with EADA Business School illustrates how two trends in the job market—the need for new competencies and skills, including digital skills, for employees at all levels, and the significance of upskilling initiatives to assist employees in adjusting to changing skill requirements and to preparing new job seekers for employment—were both intensified by the COVID-19 pandemic (Bergson-Shilcock, 2020). Vital, digital, and cognitive capacities, flexibility, adaptability, and social and emotional skills are part of this talent renewal that leaders have been summoned to be the driving force behind (Agrawal et al., 2020).

A skills-dominated market will give individuals the power to articulate their capabilities better and support employers in their talent identification. More research will be required to understand better how employers can assess and recognize skills to operate in a skill-based context (Wong et al., 2020). A world in which people expect constant job design changes to coincide is now being met with the mismatch between employees' skills and those employers seek. Professionals searching for upskilling and reskilling together with academic and non-academic educational players create a skill-up economy at the intersection of education and career paths (Dulin Salisbury, 2019). As people pursue high-tech jobs, knowledge and skill building must occur intentionally and continuously. Universities and companies have tried to bridge the gap. Many new skill-up providers, including boot camps, have sprung up to smooth the transitions between learning and career opportunities. More research is needed in this unique educational ecosystem with different players, interests, and potentially different outcomes for students and companies (Kowch, 2018).

Reskilling Will also Need to Be About Social Responsibility for Business Leaders and Educators

Companies need to invest in improved human and social capital metrics by adopting environmental, social, and governance, or ESG, metrics with renewed human capital accounting measures. Significant numbers of business leaders understand that reskilling employees, particularly in industry coalitions and public–private and academic collaborations, is cost-effective and has significant mid-to-long-term dividends—not only for their businesses but also for the benefit of society broadly. Companies expect to redeploy nearly 50% of workers internally displaced by technological automation and increase instead of making more extensive use of layoffs and automation-based labor savings as a core labor force strategy.

Emerging executive education ecosystem models can be the drivers for business schools to develop agility and readiness to reskill and upskill 4IR leaders to manage the future changing workforce. The changing nature of work is marked by international mobility, a renewed focus on organizational well-being and work–life balance, and uncertain retirement ages (Agrawal et al., 2020). Different contexts and frames of reference must be considered within reskilling/upskilling programs offered by business schools (see Crisp, 2019). The ability to motivate and lead individuals in this new and challenging reality will unavoidably require new managerial skills (Kaplan, 2018). Today's business schools must strategically design innovative education ecosystems committed to experimentation, innovation, and industry partnerships (Halkias et al., 2020; Karaboga et al., 2021).

References and Bibliography

Accenture. (2019). It's learning. Just not as we know it: How to accelerate skills acquisition in the age of intelligent technologies. Available at: Available at: https://www.accenture.com/_acnmedia/thought-leadership-assets/pdf/accenture-education-and-technology-skills-research.pdf

Adendorff, C., & Putzier, M. (2018, September 11–13). *Trends for the future* [Conference session theme address]. South African Technology Network: International Conference. 4IR The Role of Universities. KwaZulu-Natal, South Africa.

Adendorff, C., & Putzier, M. (2020). Transforming the MBA curriculum for industrial revolution 4.0. In D. Halkias, M. Neubert, P. W. Thurman, C. Adendorff, & S. Abadir (Eds.), *The innovative business school* (pp. 17–23). Routledge.

Agrawal, S., De Semet, A., Lacroix, S., & Reich, A. (2020, May 7). *To emerge stronger from the COVID-19 crisis, companies should start reskilling their workforces now.* McKinsey & Company. Available at: https://www.mckinsey.com/business-functions/organization/our-insights/to-emerge-stronger-from-the-covid-19-crisis-companies-should-start-reskilling-their-workforces-now

Alajoutsijärvi, K., Juusola, K., & Siltaoja, M. (2015). The legitimacy paradox of business schools: Losing by gaining? *Academy of Management Learning and Education, 14*(2), 277–291. 10.5465/amle.2013.0106

Alexander, M. L. (2020). *Literature review for a certificate program in 21st-century skills.* [Master's thesis, State University of New York College at Buffalo]. Digital Commons. Available at: https://digitalcommons.buffalo state.edu/creativeprojects/310/

Amdam, R. P. (2016). Executive education and the managerial revolution: The birth of executive education at Harvard business school. *Business History Review, 90*(04), 671–690. 10.1017/S0007680517000010

Arnett, T. (2014). *Why disruptive innovation matters to education.* Christensen Institute. Available at: https://www.christenseninstitute.org/blog/why-disruptive-innovation-matters-to-education/#sthash.4oUWy4xL.dpuf

Aybek, H. S. Y. (2017). Üniversite 4.0'a geçiş süreci: Kavramsal bir yaklaşım [Transition to university 4.0: A conceptual approach]. *Açıköğretim Uygulamaları ve Araştırmaları Dergisi, 3*(2), 164–176. Available at: https://earsiv.anadolu.edu.tr/xmlui/handle/11421/24667

Barber, S. (2018). A truly 'transformative' MBA: Executive education for the fourth industrial revolution. *Journal of Pedagogic Development, 8*(2). 44–55. Available at: https://www.beds.ac.uk/jpd/volume-8-issue-2/a-truly-transformative-mba-executive-education-for-the-fourth-industrial-revolution

Bennis, L., & Nanus, B. (1985) *Leaders: The strategies for taking charge.* Harper & Row.

Bergson-Shilcock, A. (2020). *Funding resilience: How public policies can support businesses in upskilling workers for a changing economy.* National Skills Coalition. Available at: https://nationalskillscoalition.org/wp-content/uploads/2020/12/08-18-2020-NSC-Funding-Resilience.pdf

Bouzidi, H. (2020). Leadership disrupted. No time for egoism! In N. Pfeffermann (Ed.), *New leadership in strategy and communication* (pp. 191–207). Springer. 10.1007/978-3-030-19681-3_14

Bradshaw, D. (Ed.). (2017). *Rethinking business education: Fit for the future.* Chartered Association of Business Schools. Available at: https://charteredabs.org/rethinking-business-education/

Brassey, J., van Dam, N., & van Witteloostuijn, A. (2019). *Advancing authentic confidence through emotional flexibility. An evidence-based playbook of insights, practices, and tools to shape your future.* LuLu Publishing.

Brende, B. (2019). *We need a reskilling revolution: Here's how to make it happen.* World Economic Forum. Available at: https://www.weforum.org/agenda/2019/04/skills-jobs-investing-in-people-inclusive-growth/

Briggs, B., & Buchholz, S. (2019). *Executive summary. Tech trends 2019.* Deloitte. Available at: https://www2.deloitte.com/insights/us/en/focus/tech-trends/2019/executive-summary.html

Browne, M., & Keeley, S. (2017). *Asking the right questions: A guide to critical thinking.* Pearson.

Bughin, J., & van Zeebroeck, N. (2017, April 6). *The best response to digital disruption.* MIT Sloan Management Review. Available at: https://sloanreview.mit.edu/article/the-right-response-to-digital-disruption/

Caporarello, L., & Manzoni, B. (2020). The role of business schools and their challenges in educating future leaders: Looking back to move forward. In N. Pfeffermann (Ed.), *New leadership in strategy and communication* (pp. 209–226). 10.1007/978-3-030-19681-3_15

Capozzi, M., Dietsch, S., Pacthod, D., & Park, M. (2020). *Rethink capabilities to emerge stronger from COVID-19.* McKinsey & Company. Available at: https://www.mckinsey.com/business-functions/mckinsey-accelerate/our-insights/rethink-capabilities-to-emerge-stronger-from-covid-19#

Capra, F. (2002). Complexity and life. *Emergence, 4*(1/2), 15–33. 10.1080/15213250.2002.9687732

Caratozzolo, P., Sirkis, G., Piloto, C., & Correa, M. (2020). Skills obsolescence and education global risks in the fourth industrial revolution. *2020 IFEES World Engineering Education Forum - Global Engineering Deans Council*, WEEF-GEDC 2020, pp. 1–5. 10.1109/WEEF-GEDC49885.2020. 9293687

Cardenas-Navia, I., & Fitzgerald, B. K. (2019). The digital dilemma: Winning and losing strategies in the digital talent race. *Industry and Higher Education*, *33*(3), 214–217. 10.1177/0950422219836669

Carella, J. (2018). *Exec ed that's anything but old school*. BizEd, AACSB International. Available at: https://bized.aacsb.edu/articles/2018/06/exec-ed-that's-anything-but-old-school

Center for the Governance of Change. (2021). *Higher education and the future of work*. Available at: https://www.ie.edu/cgc/research/higher-education-future-work/

Çeviker-Çınar, G., Mura, G., & Demirbağ-Kaplan, M. (2017). Design thinking: A new road map in business education. *Design Journal*, *20*(1), S977–S987. 10.1080/14606925.2017.1353042

Chatzinikolaou, D., & Vlados, C. (2019). *University-industry-government linkages and the helix theory on the fourth industrial revolution*. The University of Thessaly. Available at: https://papers.ssrn.com/sol3/papers. cfm?abstract_id=3400739

Chen, Y., Xu, Y., & Zhai, Q. (2019). The knowledge management functions of corporate university and their evolution: Case studies of two Chinese Corporate Universities. *Journal of Knowledge Management*, *23*(10), 2086–2112. 10.1108/JKM-04-2018-0228

Christensen, C. M. (1992). The innovator's challenge: Under-standing the influence of market environment on processes of technology development in the rigid disk drive industry. [DBA thesis. Harvard University, Cambridge, MA]. Available at: https://www.proquest.com/openview/3b6066bfa4f16aaff0baef 9838b6af38/1

Christensen, C. M., & Eyring, H. (2011). *The innovative university: Changing the DNA of higher education*. Forum for the Future of Higher Education. Available at: http://forum.mit.edu/articles/the-innovative-university-changing-the-dna-of-higher-education-2/

Christensen, C. M., Raynor, M., & McDonald, R. (2015). *What is disruptive innovation?* Harvard Business Review. Available at: https://hbr.org/2015/ 12/what-is-disruptive-innovation

Christie, P. M. J., Kwon, I.-W. G., Stoeberl, P. A., & Baumhart, R. (2003). A cross-cultural comparison of business managers' ethical attitudes: India Korea and the United States. *Journal of Business Ethics*, *46*(3), 263–287. Available at: https://0-doi-org.biblio.url.edu/10.1023/A:1025501426590

Collinson, D. (2017). Critical leadership Studies: A response to Learmonth and Morrell. *Leadership*, *13*(3), 272–284. 10.1177/1742715017694559

Cremonezi, L., & Kwen Chan, W. (2020, May 10). Financial times executive education 2020: The top 50 schools. *The Financial Times*. Available at: https://www.ft.com/content/36c1e468-8f2b-11ea-9e12-0d4655dbd44f

Crisp, A. (2019). See the future. *Global Focus: The EFMD Business Magazine, 13*(1), 4–5. Available at: https://www.globalfocusmagazine.com/see-the-future/

Cukier, W. (2020). *Return on investment: Industry leadership on upskilling and reskilling their workforce*. Public Policy Forum. Available at: http://hdl.voced.edu.au/10707/532095

Currie, G., Davies, J., & Ferlie, E. (2016). A call for university-based business schools to "lower their walls:" Collaborating with other academic departments in pursuit of social value. *Academy of Management Learning and Education, 15*(4), 742–755. 10.5465/amle.2015.0279

Currie, G., Knights, D., & Starkey, K. (2010). Introduction: A post-crisis critical reflection on business schools. *British Journal of Management, 21*(1), s1–s5. 10.1111/j.1467-8551.2009.00677.x

Dameron, S., & Durand, T. (2013). Strategies for business schools in a multi-polar world. *Education + Training, 55*(4–5), 323–335. 10.1108/00400911311325983

David, T., & Schaufelbuehl, J. M. (2015). Transatlantic influence in the shaping of business education: The origins of IMD, 1946-1990. *Business History Review, 89*(1), 75–97. 10.1017/S0007680515000069

de Vries, H., Meyer, J., Van Wassenhove, L. N., & von Bernuth, N. (2020). Strategic challenges as a learning vehicle in executive education. *International Journal of Management Education, 18*(3), Art. 100416. 10.1016/j.ijme.2020.100416

Diaz, J., & Halkias, D. (2021a). Pivoting towards an innovative executive education ecosystem in business schools. *EFMD Global Focus, 5*(3). Available at: https://www.globalfocusmagazine.com

Diaz, J., & Halkias, D. (2021b). Reskilling and upskilling 4IR leaders in business schools through an innovative executive education ecosystem: An Integrative literature review. *Social Science Research Network*. 10.2139/ssrn.3897059

Doherty, O., & Stephens, S. (2021). The skill needs of the manufacturing industry: Can higher education keep up? *Education + Training* [Ahead of print]. 10.1108/ET-05-2020-0134

Donovan, J., & Benko, C. (2016). *AT&T's talent overhaul: Can the firm really retrain hundreds of thousands of employees?* Harvard Business Review. Available at: https://hbr.org/2016/10/atts-talent-overhaul

Dorn, E., Hancock, B., Sarakatsannis, J., & Viruleg, E. (2020). *COVID-19 and student learning in the United States: The hurt could last a lifetime*. McKinsey & Company. Available at: https://www.mckinsey.com/industries/education/our-insights/covid-19-and-student-learning-in-the-united-states-the-hurt-could-last-a-lifetime

Dover, P. A., Manwani, S., & Munn, D. (2018). Creating learning solutions for executive education programs. *International Journal of Management Education, 16*(1), 80–91. 10.1016/j.ijme.2017.12.002

Dulin Salisbury, A. (2019, October 28). *As pressure to upskill grows, 5 models emerge.* Forbes. Available at: https://www.forbes.com/sites/allisondulinsa lisbury/2019/10/28/as-pressure-to-upskill-grows-5-models-emerge/?sh= 1e123bf2680c

Dunne, S., Harvey, S., & Parker, M. (2008). Speaking out: The responsibilities of management intellectuals: A survey. *Organization, 15*(2), 271–282. 10.1177/1350508407087871

Dyllick, T. (2015). Responsible management education for a sustainable world: The challenges for business schools. *Journal of Management Development, 34*(1), 16–33. Available at: https://www.emerald.com/insight/ content/doi/10.1108/JMD-02-2013-0022/full/html

Edgecliffe-Johnson, A. (2019, October 21). Are academics lagging in debate on the future of business? *The Financial Times.* Available at: https://www.ft. com/content/00c9006c-e445-11e9-b112-9624ec9edc59

EdSurge. (2016). *From skills to careers: What new job-focused learning models mean for students, educators and employers.* Available at: https://d3btwko 586hcvj.cloudfront.net/static_assets/FromSkillstoCareer.pdf

Esposito, M., Tse, T., Jean, A., & Entsminger, J. (2020). AI and higher education: Who is teaching the learners? In D. Halkias, M. Neubert, P. W. Thurman, C. Adendorff, & S. Abadir (Eds.), *The innovative business school* (pp. 99–102). Routledge. 10.4324/9780429318771

Estelami, H. (2017). The pedagogical and institutional impact of disruptive innovations in distance business education. *American Journal of Business Education, 10*(3), 97–108. 10.19030/ajbe.v10i3.9981

Etzkowitz, H., Dzisah, J., & Clouser, M. (2021). Shaping the entrepreneurial university: Two experiments and a proposal for innovation in higher education. *Industry and Higher Education,* Online. 10.1177/0950422221993421

Faix, W. G., Windisch, L., Kisgen, S., Paradowski, L., Unger, F., Bergmann, W., & Tippelt, R. (2020). A new model for state-of-the-art leadership education with performance as a driving factor for future viability. *Leadership, Education, Personality: An Interdisciplinary Journal, 2*, 59–74. 10.1365/s42681-020-00011-4

Falkenstein, M., & Snelson-Powell, A. (2020). Responsibility in business school accreditations and rankings. In D. C. Moosmayer, O. Laasch, C. Parkes, & K. G. Brown (Eds.), *The SAGE handbook of responsible management learning and education* (pp. 439–458). SAGE Publications.

Ferreri, E. (2018, September 6). *Oh, the places you could go with a Ph.D.* Duke Today. Available at: https://today.duke.edu/2018/09/oh-places-you-could-go-phd

Fung, M. (2020). Developing a robust system for upskilling and reskilling the workforce: Lessons from the skillsfuture movement in Singapore. In B. Panth & R. Maclean (Eds.), *Anticipating and preparing for emerging skills and jobs* (pp. 321–327). 10.1007/978-981-15-7018-6_39

Friedman, T. L. (2016). *Thank you for being late: An optimist's guide to thriving in the age of accelerations.* Picador.

Gagnidze, I. (2020a). *The role of entrepreneurial universities for responding the challenges of reskilling revolution.* Institutional Repository of Vadym Hetman Kyiv National Economic University, pp. 323–327. Available at: https://ir.kneu.edu.ua/handle/2010/32952

Gagnidze, I. (2020b). *The role of the education system for responding the challenges of industry 4.0.* Conference: Strategic Imperatives of Modern Management (SIMM) at KNEU, Kiev, Ukraine. Available at: https://ir.kneu.edu.ua/handle/2010/32952?locale-attribute=en

Gallagher, S. (2019, September 20). *How the value of educational credentials is and isn't changing.* Harvard Business Review. Available at: https://hbr.org/2019/09/how-the-value-of-educational-credentials-is-and-isnt-changing

García-Feijoo, M., Eizaguirre, A., & Rica-Aspiunza, A. (2020). Systematic review of sustainable-development-goal deployment in business schools. *Sustainability, 12*(1), Art. 440. 10.3390/SU12010440

Gartner. (2017, December 13). *Gartner says by 2020, artificial intelligence will create more jobs than it eliminates.* Available at: https://www.gartner.com/en/newsroom/press-releases/2017-12-13-gartner-says-by-2020-artificial-intelligence-will-create-more-jobs-than-it-eliminates

George, G., Howard-Grenville, J., Joshi, A., & Tihanyi, L. (2016). Understanding and tackling societal grand challenges through management research. *Academy of Management Journal, 59*(6), 1880–1895. 10.5465/amj.2016.4007

Giesbers, B., van den Doel, M., & Wever, K. (2021). Blended co-design of education: The case of an executive master's in security management. In G. Jacobs, I. Suojanen, K. Horton, & P. Bayerl (Eds.), *International security management. Advanced sciences and technologies for security applications* (pp. 513–529). Springer. 10.1007/978-3-030-42523-4_35

Gleason, N. W. (2018). *Higher education in the era of the fourth industrial revolution.* Springer. 10.1007/978-981-13-0194-0

Gratton, L. (2019, July 8). *New frontiers in re-skilling and upskilling.* MIT Sloan Management Review. Available at: https://sloanreview.mit.edu/article/new-frontiers-in-re-skilling-and-upskilling/

Halkias, D. (2021, October 28). *The reskilling revolution is knocking at Greece's door.* ekathimerini.com. Available at: https://www.ekathimerini.com/opinion/1170688/the-reskilling-revolution-is-knocking-at-greece-s-door/ (Accessed April1, 2022).

Halkias, D., Neubert, M., Thurman, P. W., Adendorff, C., & Abadir, S. (2020). *The innovative business school.* Routledge.

Hambrick, D. C. (2005). Just how bad are our theories? A response to Ghoshal. *Academy of Management Learning and Education, 4*(1), 104–107. 10.5465/AMLE.2005.16132585

Hancock, B., Lazaroff-Puck, K., & Rutherford, S. (2020, January 30). *Getting practical about the future of work.* McKinsey & Company. Available at: https://www.mckinsey.com/business-functions/organization/our-insights/getting-practical-about-the-future-of-work

Hartley, S. (2017). *The fuzzy and the techie: Why the liberal arts will rule the digital world.* Houghton Mifflin Harcourt.

Hazy, J. K., & Uhl-Bien, M. (2015). Towards operationalizing complexity leadership: How generative, administrative and community-building leadership practices enact organizational outcomes. *Leadership, 11*(1), 79–104. 10.1177/1742715013511483

Hill, A. (2018, January 25). Technology, globalization and the squeeze on good jobs. *The Financial Times.* Available at: https://www.ft.com/content/e66b2fa0-f7ca-11e7-a4c9-bbdefa4f210b

Horn, M. B. (2020). *Education, disrupted.* MIT Sloan Management Review. Available at: https://sloanreview.mit.edu/article/education-disrupted/

Horn, M. B., & Dunagan, A. (2018). *Innovation and quality assurance in higher education.* Christensen Institute. Available at: https://www.christenseninstitute.org/publications/quality-assurance/

Horn, M. B., & Staker, H. (2017). *Blended learning definitions.* Christensen Institute. Available at: http://www.christenseninstitute.org/blended-learning-definitions-and-models/

Huber, L., Lane, J. N., & Lakhani, K. R. (2020). *Learning with people like me: The role of age-similar peers on online business course engagement.* Harvard Business School. Available at: https://hbswk.hbs.edu/item/learning-with-people-like-me

Ifenthaler, D., & Egloffstein, M. (2020). Development and implementation of a maturity model of digital transformation. *TechTrends, 64*(2), 302–309. 10.1007/s11528-019-00457-4

Ilori, M. O., & Ajagunna, I. (2020). Re-imagining the future of education in the era of the fourth industrial revolution. *Worldwide Hospitality and Tourism Themes, 12*(1), 3–12. 10.1108/WHATT-10-2019-0066

Jack, A. (2020, May 10). Executive education must retool for the post-pandemic world. *The Financial Times.* Available at: https://www.ft.com/content/a88e72ae-8356-11ea-b872-8db45d5f6714

Jack, A. (2021a, May 9). Executive education 2021: FT survey shows what employers want. *The Financial Times.* Available at: https://www.ft.com/content/0c4a7b50-4226-45f7-8433-ed6cbdde9202

Jack, A. (2021b, May 9). Executive education 'new normal' demands different measures. *The Financial Times.* Available at: https://www.ft.com/content/bf265a1c-d2ea-4fe5-a677-79d5963a377b

Kaplan, A. (2018). A school is "a building that has four walls ... with tomorrow inside": Toward the reinvention of the business school. *Business Horizons, 61*(4), 599–608. 10.1016/j.bushor.2018.03.010

Kaplan, A. M. (2015). *European business and management.* Sage Publications.

Karaboga, T., Gurol, Y. D., Binici, C. M., & Sarp, P. (2021). Sustainable digital talent ecosystem in the new era: Impacts on businesses, governments and universities. *Istanbul Business Research, 49*(2), 360–379. 10.26650/ibr. 2020.49.0009

Kelly, R. (2019). *Constructing leadership 4.0: Swarm leadership and the fourth industrial revolution.* Springer.

Khare, A., & Hurst, D. (2017). *On the line: Business education in the digital age.* Springer. 10.1007/978-3-319-62776-2

Khurana, R., & Spender, J. C. (2012). Herbert A. Simon on what ails business schools: More than "a problem in organizational design". *Journal of Management Studies, 49*(3), 619–639. 10.1111/j.1467-6486.2011.01040.x

King, A., & Baatartogtokh, B. (2015, September 15). *How useful is the theory of disruptive innovation?* MIT Sloan Management Review. Available at: https://sloanreview.mit.edu/article/how-useful-is-the-theory-of-disruptive-innovation/

Konina, N. (2021). Introduction: At the dawn of the fourth industrial revolution—Problems and prospects. In N. Konina (Ed.), *Digital strategies in a global market* (pp. 1–12). Palgrave Macmillan. 10.1007/978-3-030-58267-8_1

Kovoor-Misra, S. (2020). The impetus for resilience and change in business education and management research. *Journal of Management Inquiry, 29*(2), 128–133. 10.1177/1056492619870871

Kowch, E. (2021). Leading transformation with digital innovations in schools and universities: Beyond adoption. In D. Ifenthaler, S. Hofhues, M. Egloffstein, & C. Helbig (Eds.), *Digital transformation of learning organizations* (pp. 145–168). Springer. 10.1007/978-3-030-55878-9_9

Kowch, E. G. (2018). Designing and leading learning ecosystems: Challenges and opportunities. *TechTrends, 62*(2), 132–134. 10.1007/s11528-018-0252-2

Kraaijenbrink, J. (2018, December 19). What does VUCA really mean? *Forbes.* Available at: https://www.forbes.com/sites/jeroenkraaijenbrink/2018/12/19/what-does-vuca-really-mean/

Laasch, O., & Gherardi, S. (2019). *Delineating and reconnecting responsible management, learning, and education (RMLE): Towards a social practices perspective of the field.* Academy of Management Annual Meeting. 10.13140/RG.2.2.23327.61606

Laasch, O., Moosmayer, D., Antonacopoulou, E., & Schaltegger, S. (2020). Constellations of transdisciplinary practices: A map and research agenda for the responsible management learning field. *Journal of Business Ethics, 162*(4), 735–757. 10.1007/s10551-020-04440-5

Librizzi, F., & Parkes, C. (2020). The United Nations-backed principles for responsible management education (PRME): A principles-based global engagement platform for higher education institutions to advance the UN sustainable development goals (SDGs). In D. C. Moosmayer, O. Laasch, C. Parkes, & K. G. Brown. (Eds.), *The SAGE handbook of responsible management learning and education* (pp. 8–27). SAGE Publications.

LeBlanc, P. J. (2018). Higher education in a VUCA world. *Change: The Magazine of Higher Learning*, *50*(3–4), 23–26. 10.1080/00091383.2018. 1507370

Li, C., & Lalani, F. (2020, April 29). The COVID-19 pandemic has changed education forever. This is how. *World Economic Forum*. Available at: https://www.weforum.org/agenda/2020/04/coronavirus-education-global-covid19-online-digital-learning/

Liu, C. (2017). International competitiveness and the fourth industrial revolution. *Entrepreneurial Business and Economics Review*, *5*(4), 111–133. 10.15678/EBER.2017.050405

Liu, X., & Murphy, L. (2020). *BILT for success: An alternative education strategy to reskill the business and technology professionals for a sustainable future.* ISCAP (Information Systems and Computing Academic Professionals). Available at: http://proc.iscap.info/2020/

Longmore, A. L., Grant, G., & Golnaraghi, G. (2018). Closing the 21st-century knowledge gap: Reconceptualizing teaching and learning to transform business education. *Journal of Transformative Education*, *16*(3), 197–219. 10.1177/1541344617738514

Lorange, P. (2012). The business school of the future: The network-based business model. *Journal of Management Development*, *31*(4), 424–430. 10.11 08/02621711211219077

Lorange, P., & Thomas, H. (2016). Pedagogical advances in business models at business schools – In the age of networks. *Journal of Management Development*, *35*(7), 889–900. 10.1108/JMD-11-2014-0150

ManpowerGroup. (2017). *2016/2017 Talent shortage survey*. Available at: https://go.manpowergroup.com/talent-shortage

Manuti, A., Pastore, S., Scardigno, A. F., Giancaspro, M. L., & Morciano, D. (2015). Formal and informal learning in the workplace: A research review. *International Journal of Training and Development*, *19*(1), 1–17. 10.1111/ijtd.12044

Manyika, J., Lund, S., Chui, M., Bughin, J., Woetzel, J., Batra, P., Ko, R., & Sanghvi, S. (2017, November 28). *Jobs lost, jobs gained: What future of work will mean for jobs, skills and wages.* McKinsey & Company. Available at: https://www.mckinsey.com/featured-insights/future-of-work/jobs-lost-jobs-gained-what-the-future-of-work-will-mean-for-jobs-skills-and-wages

Markides, C. (2006). Disruptive innovation: In need of better theory. *Journal of Product Innovation Management*, *23*(1), 19–25. 10.1111/j.1540-5885.2005. 00177.x

Markow, W., & Hughes, D. (2018). *The new foundational skills of the digital economy.* Business-Higher Education Forum and Burning Glass Technologies. Available at: https://www.burning-glass.com/wp-content/uploads/New_Foundational_Skills.pdf

McGrath, R. (2019). *Seeing around corners: How to spot inflection points in business before they happen.* Houghton Mifflin Harcourt.

McKee, S., & Gauch, D. (2020). Implications of industry 4.0 on skills development. In B. Panth & R. Maclean (Eds.), *Anticipating and preparing for emerging skills and jobs* (pp. 279–288). Springer Nature. 10.1007/978-981-15-7018-6_34

McKiernan, P., & Wilson, D. (2014). Strategic choice: Taking 'business' out of b-schools. In A. M. Pettigrew, E. Cornuel, & U. Hommel (Eds.), *The institutional development of business schools* (pp. 248–269). Oxford University Press. 10.1093/acprof:oso/9780198713364.003.0011

Millar, C. C. J. M., Groth, O., & Mahon, J. F. (2018). Management innovation in a VUCA world: Challenges and recommendations. *California Management Review, 61*(1), 5–14. 10.1177/0008125618805111

Minocha, S., Reynolds, M., & Hristov, D. (2017). Developing imaginators, not managers – How to flip the business school model. *International Journal of Management Education, 15*(3), 481–489. 10.1016/j.ijme.2017.08.002

Miotto, G., Blanco-González, A., & Díez-Martín, F. (2020). Top business schools legitimacy quest through the sustainable development goals. *Heliyon, 6*(11), Art. E05395. 10.1016/j.heliyon.2020.e05395

Mlambo, Y., Nielsen, A., & Silova, I. (2020). *Redesigning the education workforce: A design thinking approach background paper: Transforming the education workforce.* Available at: http://oro.open.ac.uk/74202/

Moldoveanu, M., & Narayandas, D. (2016). *The skills gap and the near-far problem in executive education and leadership development.* Harvard Business School Working Paper, 17. 10.13140/RG.2.2.21860.17281

Moldoveanu, M., & Narayandas, D. (2019). *The future of leadership development.* Harvard Business Review. 10.5465/amle.2006.23473214

Morgan, J. (2020). Meeting the greatest challenges for leaders of the future. *Leader to Leader, 2020*(96), 19–26. 10.1002/ltl.20500

Moules, J. (2021, February 7). FT Global MBA ranking 2021 analysis: A year of reckoning. *The Financial Times.* Available at: https://www.ft.com/content/87e53fc2-cdcb-4071-8efa-02d069a1c5b0

Murcia, M. J., Rocha, Hector O., & Birkinshaw, J. (2018). Business schools at the crossroads? A trip back from Sparta to Athens. *Journal of Business Ethics, 150*(2), 579–591. 10.1007/s10551-016-3129-3

Nakavachara, V. (2020). CEOs and graduate business education. *Journal of Education for Business, 95*(2), 73–80. 10.1080/08832323.2019.1606770

Neal, M. (2017). Learning from poverty: Why business schools should address poverty, and how they can go about it. *Academy of Management Learning and Education, 16*(1), 54–69. 10.5465/amle.2014.0369

Orlović Lovren, V., & Popović, K. (2018). Lifelong learning for sustainable development—Is adult education left behind? In W. L. Filho, M. Mifsud, & P. Pace (Eds.), *Handbook of lifelong learning for sustainable development* (pp. 1–17). Springer. 10.1007/978-3-319-63534-7_1

Pacthod, D., & Park, M. (2021, February 26). *Look for skills, not credentials: Beth Cobert on tapping into US talent.* McKinsey & Company. Available at: https://www.mckinsey.com/business-functions/mckinsey-accelerate/our-insights/look-for-skills-not-credentials-beth-cobert-on-tapping-into-us-talent

Painter-Morland, M., & Slegers, R. (2018). Strengthening "giving voice to values" in business schools by reconsidering the "invisible hand" metaphor. *Journal of Business Ethics, 147*(4), 807–819. 10.1007/s10551-017-3506-6

Paullet, K., Behling, D., & Behling, R. (2020). The role of higher education institutions in reskilling the workforce. *Issues In Information Systems, 21*(1), 49–54. 10.48009/1_iis_2020_49-54

Peters, K., Smith, R. R., & Thomas, H. (2018). *Rethinking the business models of business schools: A critical review and change agenda for the future.* Emerald Publishing Limited. 10.1108/9781787548749

Peters, K., & Thomas, H. (2011). A sustainable model for business schools? *Global. Focus: The EFMD Business Magazine, 5*(2), 24–27. Available at: https://pureportal.coventry.ac.uk/en/publications/a-sustainable-model-for-business-schools-2

Peters, K., Thomas, H., & Smith, R. R. (2018). The business of business schools. *Global Focus: The EFMD Business Magazine, 12*(1), 6–11. Available at: https://www.globalfocusmagazine.com/business-business-schools/

Positive Impact Rating. (2020). *When students rate the positive impact of business schools.* Available at: https://www.positiveimpactrating.org/report2020

Pulsipher, S. (2020, June 26). Forget bitcoin—Skills are the currency of the future. *Forbes.* Available at: https://www.forbes.com/sites/scottpulsipher/2020/06/26/forget-bitcoin-skills-are-the-currency-of-the-future/?sh=3a42eb74e766

Robinson, S. (2018, July 16). Academic view: What "sustainability" means in an MBA curriculum. *The Economist.* Available at: https://www.economist.com/node/21745910

Rotatori, D., Lee, E. J., & Sleeva, S. (2021). The evolution of the workforce during the fourth industrial revolution. *Human Resource Development International, 24*(1), 92–103. 10.1080/13678868.2020.1767453

Samuelson, J. (2021). *The six new rules of business: Creating real value in a changing world.* Berrett-Koehler Publishers.

Sawhney, M. (2021, March 26). *Reimagining executive education. What program delivery should look like post-pandemic.* Harvard Business Publishing. Available at: https://hbsp.harvard.edu/inspiring-minds/reimagining-executive-education

Scafuto, I. C., Serra, F., Guerrazzi, L., & Maccari, E. (2020). Intellectual structure of ongoing studies on business schools. *Brazilian Business Review, 17*(4), 458–487. 10.15728/BBR.2020.17.4.6

Schlegelmilch, B. B. (2020). Why business schools need radical innovations: Drivers and development trajectories. *Journal of Marketing Education, 42*(2), 93–107. 10.1177/0273475320922285

Schwab, K. (2017). *The fourth industrial revolution.* Crown Business.

Setó-Pamies, D., & Papaoikonomou, E. (2020). Sustainable development goals: A powerful framework for embedding ethics, CSR, and Sustainability in management education. *Sustainability, 12*(5), Art. 1762. 10.3390/su12051762

Shivakumar, R. (2020, February 5). Megatrends in executive education. *California Management Review, 63*(2). Available at: https://cmr.berkeley. edu/2020/02/executive-education/

Starkey, K. (2015). The strange absence of management during the current financial crisis. *Academy of Management Review, 40*(4). 10.5465/amr.2015.0109

Sukovataia, I. E., Cherkasova, Y. I., Dvinskikh, E. V., & Vitkovskaya, L. K. (2020). New approaches to the development of additional professional competences for the purposes of new economy. *Journal of Siberian Federal University. Humanities & Social Sciences, 13*(11), 1781–1792. 10.17516/ 1997-1370-0684

Strauss, V. (2017, October 18). Why we still need to study the humanities in a stem world. *The Washington Post.* Available at: https://www. washingtonpost.com/news/answer-sheet/wp/2017/10/18/why-we-still-need-to-study-the-humanities-in-a-stem-world/

Suri, N., & Hayes, J. (2020, March 9). Skills: The new currency for success. *Human Capital.* Available at: https://humancapitalonline.com/Learning-&-Development/details/782/Skills-The-New-Currency-for-Success

Telefonica. (2022, March 31). *Telefónica reinforces its Innovation and Talent Hub with the opening of the new Universitas campus* [Press release]. Available at: https://www.telefonica.com/en/communication-room/telefonica-reinforces-its-innovation-and-talent-hub-with-the-opening-of-the-new-universitas-campus/

Thomas, H., & Cornuel, E. (2012). Business schools in transition? issues of impact, legitimacy, capabilities and re-invention. *Journal of Management Development, 31*(4), 329–335. 10.1108/02621711211219095

Thomas, H., Lorange, P., & Sheth, J. (2013). Afterword: Business school futures. In H. Thomas, P. Lorange, & J. Sheth (Eds.), *The business school in the twenty-first century* (pp. 267–271). Cambridge University Press. 10.1017/ CBO9781139012119.009

Thomas, M., & Thomas, H. (2012). Using new social media and web 2.0 technologies in business school teaching and learning. *Journal of Management Development, 31*(4), 358–367. 10.1108/02621711211219013

Thomas, H., & Wilson, A. (2009). An analysis of the environment and competitive dynamics of management research. *Journal of Management Development, 28*(8), 668–684. 10.1108/02621710910985441

Torraco, R. J. (2016). Writing integrative literature reviews: Using the past and present to explore the future. *Human Resource Development Review, 15*(4), 404–428. 10.1177/1534484316671606

Trkman, P. (2019). Value proposition of business schools: More than meets the eye. *International Journal of Management Education, 17*(3), Art. 100310. 10.1016/j.ijme.2019.100310

van der Steege, M. (2017). Strategic systems coaching for leaders in turbulent times. In R. Elkington (Ed.), *Visionary leadership in a turbulent world* (pp. 229–258). Emerald Publishing Limited. 10.1108/978-1-78714-242-8201 71010

Wigmore Alvarez, A. (2019). *Making HR future proof.* Global Focus: The EFMD Business Magazine. Available at: https://www.globalfocusmagazine. com/making-hr-future-proof/

Wiles, J. (2020). *Build the workforce you need post-COVID-19.* Gartner. Available at: https://www.gartner.com/smarterwithgartner/build-the-workforce-you-need-post-covid-19

Woetzel, J., Seong, J., Leung, N., Ngai, J., Chen, L.-K., Tang, V., Agarwal, S., & Wang, B. (2021, January 21). *Reskilling China: Transforming the world's largest workforce into lifelong learners.* McKinsey & Company. Available at: https://www.mckinsey.com/featured-insights/china/reskilling-china-transforming-the-worlds-largest-workforce-into-lifelong-learners

Wong, S., Kwok, V., Kwong, T., & Lau, R. (2020). *Individuality, accessibility, and inclusivity: Applied education and lifelong learning in revolutionizing education for the 21st century.* Contribution to the Futures of Education Initiative. Our Hong Kong Foundation. Available at: https:// ourhkfoundation.org.hk/sites/default/files/media/pdf/UNESCO_submission_ 13102020.pdf

World Economic Forum. (2020). *School of the future: Defining new models of education for the fourth industrial revolution.* World Economic Forum. Available at: https://www.weforum.org/reports/schools-of-the-future-defining-new-models-of-education-for-the-fourth-industrial-revolution

Appendices

The appendices list a selection of documents used to consider the current evidence-based information on executive education ecosystem models. The integrative literature review portion of the book focuses on business school innovation, digital learning, reskilling, and upskilling the future workforce of Fourth Industrial Revolution (4IR) leaders to provide recommendations for further scholarly research, professional practice, and policymaking. Electing to focus document selection on the most representative literature without a narrow, discipline-specific focus makes linking ideas traverse sectoral and disciplinary boundaries. Therefore, this integrative review aimed to provide business school leaders, practitioners, policymakers, scholarly researchers, and other business school stakeholders with an in-depth academic and practitioner macro-level understanding of the study's central topic (see Torraco, 2016).

We performed a content analysis (Torraco, 2016) of the selected literature to obtain the most relevant knowledge on how an innovative business school ecosystem can be built to reskill and upskill 4IR leaders. The authenticity of the key ideas and themes that this analysis revealed was verified through continuous discussion with colleagues leading to their validation and/or refinement. After achieving a satisfactory degree of convergence on the key arguments extracted from the literature, we used these results to form conceptual reasoning that forms the scholarly narrative portion of our work. The work then expands the scope of the literature review by integrating insights from the extant literature on "business schools," "digital learning systems," and the "fourth industrial revolution workforce," affording in this way a greater understanding of developing an innovative executive education ecosystem model that reskills and upskills 4IR leaders to manage the future changing workforce successfully (see Caporarello & Manzoni, 2020; Fung, 2020). Such a dynamic ecosystem model for executive education is vital to educators, scholars, and policymakers to prepare for seizing existing megatrends to evolve regional economies in new directions (García-Feijoo et al., 2020).

Appendix A

Representative Literature on Innovative Business School Ecosystem

Rank	Title	Year	Author(s)	Type of Document	Citations
1	Disruptive innovation: In need of better theory	2006	Markides, C.	Journal article	1,525
2	The innovative university: Changing the DNA of higher education	2011	Christensen, C. M., & Eyring, H. J.	Book	1,435
3	What is disruptive innovation?	2015	Christensen, C. M., Raynor, M., & McDonald, R.	Journal article	40
4	Afterword: Business school futures	2013	Thomas, H., Lorange, P., & Sheth, J.	Book	81
5	How useful is the theory of disruptive innovation?	2015	King, A., & Baatartogtokh, B.	Journal article	314
6	Responsible management education for a sustainable world: The challenges for business schools	2015	Dyllick, T.	Journal article	119
7	The legitimacy paradox of business schools: Losing by gaining?	2015	Alajoutsijärvi, K., Juusola, K., & Siltaoja, M.	Journal article	109
8	A school is "a building that has four walls ... with tomorrow inside": Toward the reinvention of the business school	2018	Kaplan, A.	Journal article	21

Appendix B

Representative Literature on Digital Technology Integration in Learning Systems

Rank	Title	Year	Author(s)	Type of Document	Citations
1	Using new social media and Web 2.0 technologies in business school teaching and learning	2012	Thomas, M., & Thomas, H.	Journal article	110
2	Pedagogical advances in business models at business schools – In the age of networks	2016	Lorange, P., & Thomas, H.	Journal article	5
3	The pedagogical and institutional impact of disruptive innovations in distance business education	2017	Estelami, H.	Journal article	11
4	Designing and leading learning ecosystems: Challenges and opportunities	2018	Kowch, E.	Business report	7
5	Innovation and quality assurance in higher education	2018	Horn, M. B., & Dunagan, A.	Business report	7
6	On the line: Business education in the digital age	2018	Khare, A., & Hurst, D.	Book	7
7	How the value of educational credentials is and isn't changing	2019	Gallagher, S.	Journal article	1
8	Development and implementation of a maturity model of digital transformation	2020	Ifenthaler, D., & Egloffstein, M.	Business report	5

Appendix C

Representative Literature on Reskilling/Upskilling the Future Workforce for the 4IR

Rank	Title	Year	Author(s)	Type of Document	Citations
1	The fourth industrial revolution	2017	Schwab, K.	Book	8,314
2	Closing the 21st-century knowledge gap: Reconceptualizing teaching and learning to transform business education	2018	Longmore, A.-L., Grant, G., & Golnaraghi, G.	Journal article	21
5	New frontiers in re-skilling and upskilling	2019	Gratton, L.	Journal article	1
6	The future of leadership development	2019	Moldoveanu. M., & Narayandas, D.	Journal article	43
3	To emerge stronger from the COVID-19 crisis, companies should start reskilling their workforces now	2020	Agrawal, S., De Smet, A., Lacroix, S., & Reich, A.	Business report	10
4	Re-imagining the future of education in the era of the fourth industrial revolution	2020	Ilori, M. O., & Ajagunna, I.	Journal article	2

Index

Printed in the United States
by Baker & Taylor Publisher Services

Printed in the United States
by Baker & Taylor Publisher Services